SOCK-YARN SHAWLS II

16 Patterns for Lace Knitting

Jen Lucas

Martingale
Create with Confidence

Dedication

For my parents, Ann and Wayne

◇ ◇ ◇

Sock-Yarn Shawls II: 16 Patterns for Lace Knitting
© 2015 by Jen Lucas

Martingale®
19021 120th Ave. NE, Ste. 102
Bothell, WA 98011-9511 USA
ShopMartingale.com

Printed in China
19 18 17 16 15   8 7 6 5 4 3 2 1

Library of Congress Cataloging-in-Publication Data is available upon request.

ISBN: 978-1-60468-476-6

MISSION STATEMENT
Dedicated to providing quality products and service to inspire creativity.

CREDITS

PUBLISHER AND CHIEF VISIONARY OFFICER: Jennifer Erbe Keltner

EDITOR IN CHIEF: Mary V. Green

DESIGN DIRECTOR: Paula Schlosser

MANAGING EDITOR: Karen Costello Soltys

ACQUISITIONS EDITOR: Karen M. Burns

TECHNICAL EDITOR: Amy Polcyn

COPY EDITOR: Marcy Heffernan

PRODUCTION MANAGER: Regina Girard

COVER AND INTERIOR DESIGNER: Adrienne Smitke

PHOTOGRAPHER: Brent Kane

ILLUSTRATOR: Kathryn Conway

Contents

Introduction

When it came time to start thinking about my second book, I just couldn't get shawls out of my head. My first book, *Sock-Yarn Shawls* (Martingale, 2013), contains lots of great patterns for small shawls, and those are still the types of projects I like to knit. But I kept thinking about all the shapes and sizes of shawls that I didn't hit in that first book. My new obsession with attach-as-you-go lace borders? Nowhere to be found in book one. Huge circular pi shawl to stop knitters in their tracks at a convention? Nope.

Sock-yarn shawls don't need to be made from just one skein of yarn. Sure, the one-skein projects are great for quick knits and perfect for wearing under your coat on a blustery winter day, but sometimes you want something more substantial. Since my sock-yarn stash (and let's be honest, yours too) has only grown since *Sock-Yarn Shawls* first hit yarn shops and bookstores, it made sense to explore knitting shawls that use more yarn. Maybe that will help me get the yarn stash under control!

The patterns in this book are organized into three sections—Small Shawls, Midsize Shawls, and Large Shawls. In the first section, the shawls can be knit with one skein of sock yarn, using 450 yards or less of yarn. This is a great start for new shawl knitters, as the projects don't require a lot of time or yarn to complete. If you enjoyed the patterns from the first book, you are sure to find something you will love in this section.

The second section features patterns that require a little more yarn. Some of the patterns require two skeins of the same yarn while others give you the freedom to play around with yarn and color choices, as you'll be using two different-colored yarns. The projects in this section take between 450 and 900 yards of yarn.

Finally, in Large Shawls, you will find shawls that require 900 yards or more of yarn to complete. Here you'll find beautiful multicolored shawls and circular pi shawls. If you're looking for a challenge with a beautiful cozy shawl as a prize, then start here. The patterns in this section are a little more difficult, but the hard work will be worth it! You'll be turning heads with these projects.

While the patterns are split into sections by size, maybe you want to change the size of your shawl and make it larger or smaller. In a few of the patterns you will find a tip box on how to adjust the size of the shawl if you wish.

I hope you enjoy the patterns in this book. Let the sock-yarn-shawl knitting obsession continue!

Choosing the Right Yarn

In this swatch, the skeins were alternated every two rows, blending the slight color differences.

In this swatch, skeins were switched halfway through, making for a noticeable color change.

A Note about Gauge

All gauges listed in this book are based on a washed, blocked swatch. Take time to check that gauge so you won't run out of yarn!

You're ready to knit your sock-yarn shawl, but how do you pick the right yarn? In *Sock-Yarn Shawls,* I discussed some considerations for choosing yarn, which are just as important for knitting the projects in this book.

Yardage is probably the most important consideration when choosing your yarn. Lots of sock yarn is hand-dyed, making it nearly impossible to purchase another matching skein if you run out. Some types have less than 400 yards, while others contain as much as 450 yards. So, just like with any project, make sure you check the yarn label for yardage (and other details) before you buy.

It's also important to consider the color of the yarn. Variegated yarn is beautiful, but not always the best choice when it comes to lace projects. If the shawl contains a very small lace motif, you can often get away with a more variegated yarn. However, if the pattern has a large lace motif, the yarn and stitch pattern are going to fight each other and it will be difficult to see the lace pattern through the yarn.

For larger projects that use one color of yarn, you'll want to consider alternating skeins of yarn for the duration of the project, especially when using a hand-dyed yarn. For example, the Lycopod (page 57) and Harvest (page 63) shawls use beautiful hand-dyed yarns. But even when these yarns are dyed at the same time, they don't always match perfectly. Such is the nature of hand-dyeing. To ensure your shawl looks like one color throughout, switch skeins every two rows. That way, the slight differences in skeins blend together subtly, rather than creating a noticeable difference when you switch skeins midway through the project. In the swatches at left, one was knit by alternating skeins of hand-dyed yarn, and the other was knit by switching to a new skein halfway through. See the difference?

So, dig into that sock-yarn stash of yours and find a skein or two to start your shawl knitting!

Using—and Moving— Stitch Markers

When it comes to repeating a set of stitches across a row, some knitters find it helpful to place a stitch marker after each repeat. You can end up with a lot of stitch markers on the needle when you do this, but it can help you keep track of where you are in the pattern. However, placing a stitch marker at each lace repeat in the row can cause issues, depending on how the lace is set up. In some cases, you may have to "borrow a stitch" from the next repeat in order to complete the repeat you are working. This can become a little confusing, so let's look at an example.

When working the following chart, you'll have to borrow a stitch from the next repeat when each repeat is split up with stitch markers.

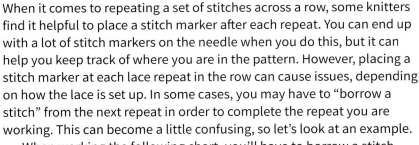

Repeat = 9 sts

Three stitches are needed to complete the double decrease, but there are only two stitches before the marker.

Legend

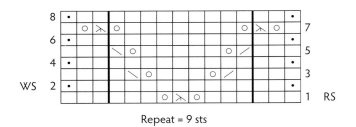

☐ K on RS, P on WS   ⊼ Sk2p

• P on RS, K on WS   ⟍ Ssk

○ YO   ⟋ K2tog

When working the first row of the pattern, place the stitch markers at each repeat indicated by the bold vertical lines. When working the next five rows, just slip the markers along the way. When you get to row 7, it will be time to borrow a stitch. At the first double decrease you will only have two stitches left before the marker, but you need three stitches in order to complete that stitch (top photo).

Remove the stitch marker, complete the double-decrease stitch, and then place the stitch marker on the right needle (bottom photo).

Repeat this process across the row, moving the stitch marker at each repeat.

For patterns in this book where the stitch markers would need to be moved, you'll find details in the Pattern Notes for that particular project. Whether you decide to use lots of stitch markers or none at all is entirely up to you. If you do choose to add stitch markers at each repeat, hopefully this explanation of how to move them around when necessary will lead you to successful lace knitting.

The marker was removed, the stitch was completed, and the marker was placed back on the needle.

Small Shawls

Have just one skein of precious sock yarn? In this section, you'll find patterns that take a single skein to complete. All the projects are designed to use 450 yards of yarn or less.

JUNIPER

The Juniper shawl is crescent shaped, knit from the lace edge and worked upward to the neck edge. Short rows in the stockinette body of the shawl create the curved shape.

"Juniper," designed and knitted by author

Skill Level: Intermediate ◇ ◇ ◇ ◇
Finished Measurements: 12" x 46"

MATERIALS

1 skein of BFL Sock from Huckleberry Knits (80% merino, 20% nylon; 100 g; 420 yds) in color Garnet **1**

US size 5 (3.75 mm) circular needle, 24" cable or longer, or size needed to obtain gauge

Tapestry needle

Blocking wires and/or blocking pins

GAUGE

18 sts and 32 rows = 4" in St st

PATTERN NOTES

Charts A and B are on page 11. If you prefer to follow written instructions for the charted material, see "Written Instructions for Charts" on page 10.

INSTRUCTIONS

CO 349 sts. Knit 2 rows. Work rows 1–8 of chart A 3 times. Then work rows 1–8 of chart B. (273 sts)

Short-Row Section 1

Row 1 (RS): K141, turn work. (132 sts unworked)

Row 2 (WS): P9, turn work. (132 sts unworked)

Row 3: K8, ssk, K3, turn work. (128 sts unworked; 272 sts total)

Row 4: P11, P2tog, P3, turn work. (128 sts unworked; 271 sts total)

Row 5: Knit to 1 st before gap (1 st before previous turning point), ssk, K3, turn work.

Row 6: Purl to 1 st before gap (1 st before previous turning point), P2tog, P3, turn work.

Work rows 5 and 6 another 15 times. (64 sts rem unworked on each end of shawl; 239 sts total)

Short-Row Section 2

Row 1 (RS): Knit to 1 st before gap (1 st before previous turning point), ssk, K7, turn work.

Row 2 (WS): Purl to 1 st before gap (1 st before previous turning point), P2tog, P7, turn work.

Work rows 1 and 2 another 6 times. (8 sts rem unworked on each end of shawl; 225 sts total)

Rows 3 and 4: Knit to 1 st before gap (1 st before previous turning point), ssk, K7, turn work. All sts have been worked. (223 sts)

FINISHING

BO loosely knitwise as described on page 77. With tapestry needle, weave in ends. Using blocking wires or pins, block to finished measurements.

WRITTEN INSTRUCTIONS FOR CHARTS

If you prefer to follow row-by-row written instructions rather than a chart, use the instructions below.

Chart A

Row 1 (RS): K2, P1, *K1tbl, P1, K2tog, K1, YO, K1, K2tog, (K1, YO) twice, K1, ssk, K1, YO, K1, ssk, P1; rep from * to last 4 sts, K1tbl, P1, K2.

Row 2 (WS): K3, P1tbl, *K1, P15, K1, P1tbl; rep from * to last 3 sts, K3.

Row 3: K2, P1, *K1tbl, P1, YO, ssk, K1, K2tog, K1, YO, K3, YO, K1, ssk, K1, K2tog, YO, P1; rep from * to last 4 sts, K1tbl, P1, K2.

Row 4: K3, P1tbl, *K2, P13, K2, P1tbl; rep from * to last 3 sts, K3.

Row 5: K2, P1, *K1tbl, P2, YO, sk2p, K1, YO, K5, YO, K1, sk2p, YO, P2; rep from * to last 4 sts, K1tbl, P1, K2.

Row 6: K3, P1tbl, *K2, P13, K2, P1tbl; rep from * to last 3 sts, K3.

Row 7: K2, P1, *K1tbl, P2, K2tog, K1, YO, K7, YO, K1, ssk, P2; rep from * to last 4 sts, K1tbl, P1, K2.

Row 8: K3, P1tbl, *K2, P13, K2, P1tbl; rep from * to last 3 sts, K3.

Rep rows 1–8 for patt.

Chart B

Row 1 (RS): K2, P1, *K1tbl, P1, K2tog, K1, YO, K1, K2tog, (K1, YO) twice, K1, ssk, K1, YO, K1, ssk, P1; rep from * to last 4 sts, K1tbl, P1, K2.

Row 2 (WS): K3, P1tbl, *K1, P15, K1, P1tbl; rep from * to last 3 sts, K3.

The V-shaped lace pattern creates a beautiful scalloped edge on the shawl.

Row 3: K2, P1, *K1tbl, P1, YO, ssk, K1, K2tog, K1, YO, K3, YO, K1, ssk, K1, K2tog, YO, P1; rep from * to last 4 sts, K1tbl, P1, K2.

Row 4: K3, P1tbl, *K1, P15, K1, P1tbl; rep from * to last 3 sts, K3.

Row 5: K2, P1, *K1tbl, P1, K1, sk2p, K1, YO, K5, YO, K1, sk2p, K1, P1; rep from * to last 4 sts, K1tbl, P1, K2.

Row 6: K3, P1tbl, *K1, P13, K1, P1tbl; rep from * to last 3 sts, K3.

Row 7: K2, P1, *K1tbl, P1, K2tog, K1, YO, K1, K2tog, K1, ssk, K1, YO, K1, ssk, P1; rep from * to last 4 sts, K1tbl, P1, K2.

Row 8: K3, P1tbl, *K1, P11, K1, P1tbl; rep from * to last 3 sts, K3.

Juniper Chart A

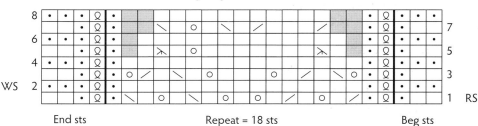

End sts Repeat = 18 sts Beg sts

Juniper Chart B

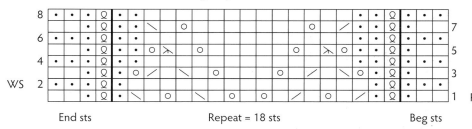

End sts Repeat = 18 sts Beg sts
(decreases to 16 sts on row 5 and to 14 sts on row 7)

Legend

☐ K on RS, P on WS	○ YO
• P on RS, K on WS	╲ Ssk
Ω K1tbl on RS, P1tbl on WS	⋏ Sk2p
╱ K2tog	▨ No stitch

CINDER

Here's a traditional top-down triangle shawl, with a twist—once the lace begins, it's time to ditch the center stitch and work a lovely lace pattern that looks like stacked bricks.

"Cinder," designed by author and knitted by Jennifer Sinnott

Skill Level: Easy ◈ ◈ ◇ ◇

Finished Measurements: 17" x 50"

MATERIALS

1 skein of Adorn Sock from Three Irish Girls (80% merino, 20% nylon; 100 g; 430 yds) in color Salt Spray **1**

US size 4 (3.5 mm) circular needle, 24" cable or longer, or size needed to obtain gauge

4 stitch markers

Tapestry needle

Blocking wires and/or blocking pins

GAUGE

22 sts and 32 rows = 4" in St st

PATTERN NOTES

Charts A and B are on page 15. If you prefer to follow written instructions for the charted material, see "Written Instructions for Charts" on page 14.

Make It Bigger!

With additional yarn, continue to repeat charts A and B, ending with row 7 of chart B. Work the last 3 rows of lace edge as written.

FINISHING

BO loosely knitwise as described on page 77. With tapestry needle, weave in ends. Using blocking wires or pins, block to finished measurements.

WRITTEN INSTRUCTIONS FOR CHARTS

If you prefer to follow row-by-row written instructions rather than a chart, use the instructions below.

Chart A

Row 1 (RS): K3, YO, knit to last 3 sts, YO, K3.

Row 2 and all even-numbered rows (WS): K4, YO, purl to last 4 sts, YO, K4.

Row 3: K3, YO, K2, *K3, YO, sk2p, YO; rep from * to last 8 sts, K5, YO, K3.

Row 5: K3, YO, knit to last 3 sts, YO, K3.

Row 7: K3, YO, K1, YO, K2tog, YO, K3, *YO, sk2p, YO, K3; rep from * to last 12 sts, YO, sk2p, YO, K3, YO, ssk, YO, K1, YO, K3.

Row 8: K4, YO, purl to last 4 sts, YO, K4.

INSTRUCTIONS

Begin shawl by working set-up rows as follows.

Work tab CO (page 76) as foll: CO 3 sts. Knit 6 rows. Turn work 90° and pick up 3 sts along edge. Turn work 90° and pick up 3 sts from CO edge. (9 sts total)

Body of Shawl

Row 1 (RS): K3, PM, YO, K1, YO, PM, K1 (this is the center st), PM, YO, K1, YO, PM, K3. (13 sts)

Row 2 (WS): K3, purl to last 3 sts slipping markers along the way, K3.

Row 3: K3, SM, YO, knit to next marker, YO, SM, K1, SM, YO, knit to last marker, YO, SM, K3. (17 sts)

Work rows 2 and 3 another 37 times. Rep row 2 once more. (165 sts)

Next row (RS): K3, SM, YO, K2, M1, knit to next marker, YO, SM, K1, SM, YO, knit to 2 sts before last marker, M1, K2, YO, SM, K3. (171 sts)

Next row (WS): K3, purl to last 3 sts removing markers along the way, K3.

Lace Edge

Work chart A. (189 sts)

Work chart B. (207 sts)

Work chart A. (225 sts)

Work chart B. (243 sts)

Work chart A. (261 sts)

Work rows 1–7 of chart B. (277 sts)

Next row (WS): K2, K1f&b, knit to end. (278 sts)

Next row (RS): K1, *YO twice, sk2p; rep from * to last st, YO twice, K1.

Next row: K1, *(K1, P1) twice into double YO, K1; rep from * to last 3 sts, (K1, P1) twice into double YO, K1.

Chart B

Row 1 (RS): K3, YO, knit to last 3 sts, YO, K3.

Row 2 and all even-numbered rows (WS): K4, YO, purl to last 4 sts, YO, K4.

Row 3: K3, YO, K2, *YO, sk2p, YO, K3; rep from * to last 8 sts, YO, sk2p, YO, K2, YO, K3.

Row 5: K3, YO, knit to last 3 sts, YO, K3.

Row 7: K3, YO, K4, YO, K2tog, YO, *K3, YO, sk2p, YO; rep from * to last 12 sts, K3, YO, ssk, YO, K4, YO, K3.

Row 8: K4, YO, purl to last 4 sts, YO, K4.

The extra yarnovers at the edge of the shawl add interest to the simple lace pattern.

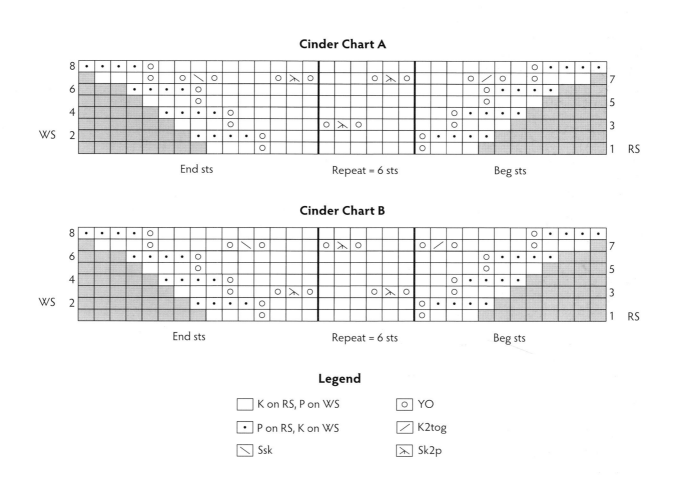

Cinder Chart A

Cinder Chart B

Legend

☐	K on RS, P on WS	○	YO
•	P on RS, K on WS	╱	K2tog
╲	Ssk	⋌	Sk2p

ZUZU

Zuzu is a reversible kerchief-style shawlette, perfect for the knitter looking for an easy, quick knit. It starts at the bottom and is worked upward, with easy short rows added to give the kerchief a little shape and drape.

"Zuzu," designed by author and knitted by Cathy Rusk

Skill Level: Easy ◆ ◆ ◇ ◇
Finished Measurements: 17" x 46"

MATERIALS

1 skein of Breathless from Shalimar Yarns (75% superwash merino, 15% cashmere, 10% silk; 100 g; 420 yds) in color Primula (**1**)
US size 5 (3.75 mm) circular needle, 24" cable or longer, or size needed to obtain gauge
Tapestry needle
Blocking wires and/or blocking pins

GAUGE

22 sts and 20 rows = 4" in garter st

PATTERN NOTES

This shawlette is reversible. There is no right or wrong side; however, you may find it helpful to mark one side of the shawl and note whether odd or even rows are worked on that side.

INSTRUCTIONS

CO 4 sts.

Row 1: (K1, YO) 3 times, K1. (7 sts)

Row 2: Knit all sts.

Row 3: (K1, YO) 6 times, K1. (13 sts)

Row 4: Knit all sts.

Row 5: (K1, YO) twice, (K2tog, YO) to last st, K1. (15 sts)

Work row 5 another 64 times. (143 sts)

Row 6: (K1, YO) twice, knit to end. (145 sts)

Work row 6 another 37 times. (219 sts)

Short-Row Section

Row 1: K114, turn work. (105 sts unworked)

Row 2: K9, turn work. (105 sts unworked)

Row 3: K8, ssk, K4, turn work. (100 sts unworked; 218 sts total)

Row 4: K12, ssk, K4, turn work. (100 sts unworked; 217 sts total)

Row 5: Knit to 1 st before gap (1 st before previous turning point), ssk, K4, turn work.

Work row 5 another 39 times. All sts worked. Knit 4 rows. (177 sts)

FINISHING

BO loosely knitwise as described on page 77. With tapestry needle, weave in ends. Using blocking wires or pins, block to finished measurements.

The reversible mesh pattern is worked the same on both sides of the shawl.

WAVELAND

This shawl starts at the top center and is worked outward in garter stitch. After the body of the shawl is complete, additional stitches are cast on to work the lace border perpendicularly to the body—a fun, quick knit!

"Waveland," designed by author and knitted by Vickie Zinnel

Skill Level: Intermediate ◇ ◇ ◇ ◇
Finished Measurements: 14" x 54"

MATERIALS

1 skein of Entice MCN from Hazel Knits (70% superwash merino, 20% cashmere, 10% nylon; 115 g; 400 yds) in color In the Clover ⟨**1**⟩
US size 5 (3.75 mm) circular needle, 24" cable or longer, or size needed to obtain gauge
Tapestry needle
Blocking wires and/or blocking pins

GAUGE

20 sts and 24 rows = 4" in garter st

With a lace edge pattern that's so easy, no chart is necessary.

INSTRUCTIONS

Begin shawl by working set-up rows as follows.

Work tab CO (page 76) as foll: CO 3 sts. Knit 8 rows. Turn work 90° and pick up 4 sts along the edge. Turn work 90° and pick up 3 sts from CO edge. (10 sts total)

Body of Shawl

Row 1 (RS): K2, YO, K1, YO, K4, YO, K1, YO, K2. (14 sts)

Row 2 (WS): Knit all sts.

Row 3: K2, (YO, K1) 3 times, YO, K4, YO, (K1, YO) 3 times, K2. (22 sts)

Row 4: Knit all sts.

Row 5: K2, YO, K1, YO, knit to last 3 sts, YO, K1, YO, K2. (26 sts)

Work rows 4 and 5 another 50 times. Rep row 4 once more. (226 sts)

Lace Edge

Using knitted cast on (page 76), CO 15 sts.

Row 1 (RS): K14, ssk last border st with first body st on left needle.

Row 2 (WS): Sl 1 wyib, K14.

Work rows 1 and 2 once more.

Row 3: K3, (K2tog, YO) 4 times, K3, ssk last border st with first body st on left needle.

Row 4: Sl 1 wyib, K14.

Row 5: K4, (K2tog, YO) 4 times, K2, ssk last border st with first body st on left needle.

Row 6: Sl 1 wyib, K14.

Work rows 3–6 another 110 times. (2 sts from body of shawl remain)

Row 7: K14, ssk last border st with first body st on left needle.

Row 8: Sl 1 wyib, K14.

Work rows 7 and 8 once more.

FINISHING

BO loosely knitwise as described on page 77. With tapestry needle, weave in ends. Using blocking wires or pins, block to finished measurements.

JASMINE

To me, the interlocking lace pattern at the edge of this bottom-up short-row shawl looks like a row of perfume bottles. Maybe one has a genie in it?

"Jasmine," designed by author and knitted by Gail Nebl

Skill Level: Intermediate ◇ ◇ ◇ ◇
Finished Measurements: 9" x 56"

MATERIALS

1 skein of Djinni Sock from Dragonfly Fibers (80% superwash merino, 10% cashmere, 10% nylon; 100 g; 420 yds) in color Celery Seed **1**

US size 4 (3.5 mm) circular needle, 24" cable or longer, or size needed to obtain gauge

Tapestry needle

Blocking wires and/or blocking pins

GAUGE

20 sts and 36 rows = 4" in St st

PATTERN NOTES

The chart is on page 25. If you prefer to follow written instructions for the charted material, see "Written Instructions for Chart" on page 24.

If using stitch markers to mark each 10-stitch repeat in the chart, the stitch markers will need to be rearranged on rows 9 and 17. See page 6 for more information on how to move markers.

INSTRUCTIONS

CO 293 sts. Knit 1 row. Work chart once.

Next row (RS): K2, K2tog twice, knit to last 6 sts, K2tog twice, K2. (289 sts)

Next row (WS): K3, purl to last 3 sts, K3.

Short-Row Section 1

Row 1 (RS): K149, turn work. (140 sts unworked)

Row 2 (WS): P9, turn work. (140 sts unworked)

Row 3: K8, ssk, K4, turn work. (135 sts unworked; 288 sts total)

Row 4: P12, P2tog, P4, turn work. (135 sts unworked; 287 sts total)

Row 5: Knit to 1 st before gap (1 st before previous turning point), ssk, K4, turn work.

Row 6: Purl to 1 st before gap (1 st before previous turning point), P2tog, P4, turn work.

Work rows 5 and 6 another 18 times. (40 sts unworked on each side; 249 sts total)

Short-Row Section 2

Row 1 (RS): Knit to 1 st before gap (1 st before previous turning point), ssk, K9, turn work.

Row 2 (WS): Purl to 1 st before gap (1 st before previous turning point), P2tog, P9, turn work.

Work rows 1 and 2 another 3 times. (All sts have been worked; 241 sts total)

Garter-Stitch Edge

Knit 6 rows.

FINISHING

BO loosely knitwise as described on page 77. With tapestry needle, weave in ends. Using blocking wires or pins, block to finished measurements.

WRITTEN INSTRUCTIONS FOR CHART

If you prefer to follow row-by-row written instructions rather than a chart, use the instructions below.

Row 1 (RS): K6, *K4, K2tog, YO, K4; rep from * to last 7 sts, K7.

Row 2 and all even-numbered rows (WS): K3, purl to last 3 sts, K3.

Row 3: K6, *K3, K2tog, YO, K1, YO, ssk, K2; rep from * to last 7 sts, K7.

Row 5: K6, *K2, K2tog, YO, K3, YO, ssk, K1; rep from * to last 7 sts, K7.

Row 7: K6, *K1, K2tog, YO, K5, YO, ssk; rep from * to last 7 sts, K7.

Row 9: K5, YO, *sk2p, YO, K7, YO; rep from * to last 8 sts, sk2p, YO, K5.

Row 11: K6, *YO, ssk, K8; rep from * to last 7 sts, YO, ssk, K5.

Row 13: K4, K2tog, YO, *K1, YO, ssk, K5, K2tog, YO; rep from * to last 7 sts, K1, YO, ssk, K4.

Row 15: K3, K2tog, YO, K1, *K2, YO, ssk, K3, K2tog, YO, K1; rep from * to last 7 sts, K2, YO, ssk, K3.

Row 17: K5, YO, *sk2p, YO, K7, YO; rep from * to last 8 sts, sk2p, YO, K5.

Row 19: K6, *YO, ssk, K8; rep from * to last 7 sts, YO, ssk, K5.

Row 21: K6, *K1, YO, ssk, K5, K2tog, YO; rep from * to last 7 sts, K7.

Row 23: K6, *K2, YO, ssk, K3, K2tog, YO, K1; rep from * to last 7 sts, K7.

Row 25: K6, *K3, YO, ssk, K1, K2tog, YO, K2; rep from * to last 7 sts, K7.

Row 27: K6, *K4, YO, sk2p, YO, K3; rep from * to last 7 sts, K7.

Row 28: K3, purl to last 3 sts, K3.

Jasmine Chart

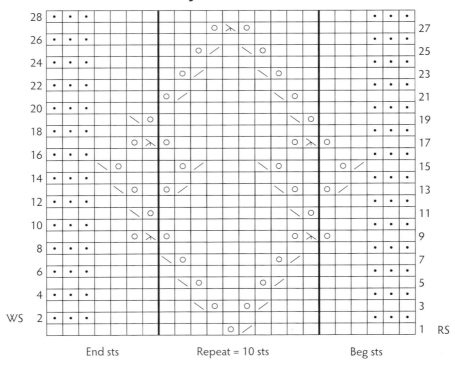

WS — RS

End sts   Repeat = 10 sts   Beg sts

Legend

☐ K on RS, P on WS	⊙ YO
• P on RS, K on WS	╱ K2tog
╲ Ssk	⋏ Sk2p

MONARDA

Featuring garter stitch and lace, this shawl offers lots to love. Started from the top center and worked outward, this addictive lace pattern will leave you wanting to make more than one.

"Monarda," designed and knitted by author

Skill Level: Easy ◇◇◇◇
Finished Measurements: 18" x 56"

MATERIALS

1 skein of Tosh Sock from Madelintosh (100% superwash merino wool; 100 g; 395 yds) in color Posy (**1**)

US size 4 (3.5 mm) circular needle, 24" cable or longer, or size needed to obtain gauge

Tapestry needle

Blocking wires and/or blocking pins

GAUGE

20 sts and 28 rows = 4" in St st

PATTERN NOTES

Charts A, B, and C are on page 30. If you prefer to follow written instructions for the charted material, see "Written Instructions for Charts" on page 28.

If using stitch markers to mark each pattern repeat, on some rows the stitch markers will have to be rearranged. For chart B, the markers will move on row 9. See page 6 for more information on how to move the markers.

INSTRUCTIONS

Begin shawl by working set-up rows as follows.

CO 5 sts.

Row 1 (RS): (K1, K1f&b) twice, K1. (7 sts)

Row 2 (WS): K2, (YO, K1) 3 times, YO, K2. (11 sts)

Row 3: K2, YO, K1, YO, ssk, K1, K2tog, YO, K1, YO, K2. (13 sts)

Row 4: K2, YO, purl to last 2 sts, YO, K2. (15 sts)

Row 5: K2, YO, K4, YO, sk2p, YO, K4, YO, K2. (17 sts)

Row 6: K2, YO, K2, purl to last 4 sts, K2, YO, K2. (19 sts)

Body of Shawl

Work chart A 7 times. (215 sts)

Work chart B once. (243 sts)

Work chart C once. (253 sts)

Stitch Count

First rep of chart A	47 sts
Second rep of chart A	75 sts
Third rep of chart A	103 sts
Fourth rep of chart A	131 sts
Fifth rep of chart A	159 sts
Sixth rep of chart A	187 sts
Seventh rep of chart A	215 sts

Make It Bigger!

With additional yarn, continue to repeat chart A before moving on to chart B.

FINISHING

BO loosely purlwise as described on page 78. With tapestry needle, weave in ends. Using blocking wires or pins, block to finished measurements.

WRITTEN INSTRUCTIONS FOR CHARTS

If you prefer to follow row-by-row written instructions rather than a chart, use the instructions below.

Chart A

Row 1 (RS): K2, YO, K1, *K2, ssk, K2, YO, K1, YO, K2, K2tog, K3; rep from * to last 2 sts, YO, K2.

Row 2 (WS): K2, YO, K1, *K3, P9, K2; rep from * to last 4 sts, K2, YO, K2.

Row 3: K2, YO, K3, *K2, ssk, K2, YO, K1, YO, K2, K2tog, K3; rep from * to last 4 sts, K2, YO, K2.

Row 4: K2, YO, P1, K2, *K3, P9, K2; rep from * to last 6 sts, K3, P1, YO, K2.

Row 5: K2, YO, K5, *K2, ssk, K2, YO, K1, YO, K2, K2tog, K3; rep from * to last 6 sts, K4, YO, K2.

Row 6: K2, YO, P3, K2, *K3, P9, K2; rep from * to last 8 sts, K3, P3, YO, K2.

Row 7: K2, YO, K2, K2tog, YO, K3, *K2, YO, ssk, K5, K2tog, YO, K3; rep from * to last 8 sts, K2, YO, ssk, K2, YO, K2.

Row 8: K2, YO, P5, K2, *K3, P9, K2; rep from * to last 10 sts, K3, P5, YO, K2.

Row 9: K2, YO, K3, K2tog, YO, K4, *K3, YO, ssk, K3, K2tog, YO, K4; rep from * to last 10 sts, K3, YO, ssk, K3, YO, K2.

Row 10: K2, YO, P7, K2, *K3, P9, K2; rep from * to last 12 sts, K3, P7, YO, K2.

Row 11: K2, YO, K1, YO, ssk, K1, K2tog, YO, K5, *K4, YO, ssk, K1, K2tog, YO, K5; rep from * to last 12 sts, K4, YO, ssk, K1, K2tog, YO, K1, YO, K2.

Row 12: K2, YO, P9, K2, *K3, P9, K2; rep from * to last 14 sts, K3, P9, YO, K2.

Row 13: K2, YO, K4, YO, sk2p, YO, K6, *K5, YO, sk2p, YO, K6; rep from * to last 14 sts, K5, YO, sk2p, YO, K4, YO, K2.

Row 14: K2, YO, K2, P9, K2, *K3, P9, K2; rep from * to last 16 sts, K3, P9, K2, YO, K2.

Rep rows 1–14 for patt.

Chart B

Row 1 (RS): K2, YO, K1, *K3, K2tog, YO, K3, YO, ssk, K4; rep from * to last 2 sts, YO, K2.

Row 2 (WS): K2, YO, K1, *K3, P9, K2; rep from * to last 4 sts, K2, YO, K2.

Row 3: K2, YO, K3, *K2, K2tog, YO, K5, YO, ssk, K3; rep from * to last 4 sts, K2, YO, K2.

Mix garter and lace stitches together for a favorite combination!

Row 4: K2, YO, P1, K2, *K3, P9, K2; rep from * to last 6 sts, K3, P1, YO, K2.

Row 5: K2, YO, K1, YO, ssk, K2, *K1, K2tog, YO, K7, YO, ssk, K2; rep from * to last 6 sts, K1, K2tog, YO, K1, YO, K2.

Row 6: K2, YO, P4, K1, *K2, P11, K1; rep from * to last 8 sts, K2, P4, YO, K2.

Row 7: K2, YO, K4, YO, ssk, K1, *K2tog, YO, K9, YO, ssk, K1; rep from * to last 8 sts, K2tog, YO, K4, YO, K2.

Row 8: K2, YO, P7, *K1, P13; rep from * to last 10 sts, K1, P7, YO, K2.

Row 9: K2, YO, K7, YO, sk2p, *YO, K11, YO, sk2p; rep from * to last 9 sts, YO, K7, YO, K2.

Row 10: K2, YO, purl to last 2 sts, YO, K2.

Row 11: K2, YO, K3, K2tog, K5, YO, K1, *YO, K5, sk2p, K5, YO, K1; rep from * to last 12 sts, YO, K5, ssk, K3, YO, K2.

Row 12: K2, YO, purl to last 2 sts, YO, K2.

Row 13: K2, YO, K5, K2tog, K5, YO, K1, *YO, K5, sk2p, K5, YO, K1; rep from * to last 14 sts, YO, K5, ssk, K5, YO, K2.

Row 14: K2, YO, purl to last 2 sts, YO, K2.

Chart C

Row 1 (RS): K2, YO, K1, *YO, K5, sk2p, K5, YO, K1; rep from * to last 2 sts, YO, K2.

Row 2 (WS): K2, YO, purl to last 2 sts, YO, K2.

Row 3: K2, YO, K3, *YO, K5, sk2p, K5, YO, K1; rep from * to last 4 sts, K2, YO, K2.

Row 4: K2, YO, purl to last 2 sts, YO, K2.

Row 5: K2, YO, K5, *YO, K5, sk2p, K5, YO, K1; rep from * to last 6 sts, K4, YO, K2.

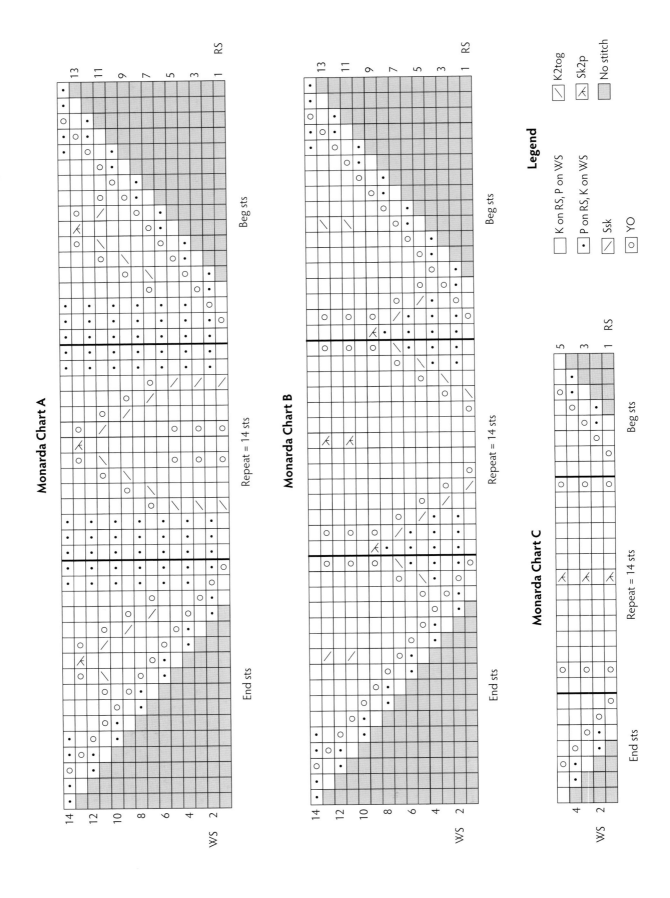

Monarda Chart A

Monarda Chart B

Monarda Chart C

Legend

	K on RS, P on WS		K2tog
•	P on RS, K on WS		Sk2p
/	Ssk		No stitch
○	YO		

Midsize Shawls

Sometimes sock-yarn shawls require a little extra yarn for a bit more size and substance. The projects in this section use up to 900 yards and are perfect for when you want to knit something you can snuggle up in.

SPARROW

Start with a circular pi shawl construction and then transition into increases typically seen in triangular shawls. The combination creates a shawl that will drape beautifully over your shoulders.

"Sparrow," designed and knitted by author

Skill Level: Experienced ◇ ◇ ◇ ◇
Finished Measurements: 24" x 52"

MATERIALS

2 skeins of Entice MCN from Hazel Knits (70% superwash merino, 20% cashmere, 10% nylon; 100 g; 400 yds) in color Lichen (**1**)

US size 4 (3.5 mm) circular needle, 24" cable or longer, or size needed to obtain gauge

6 stitch markers

Tapestry needle

Blocking wires and/or blocking pins

GAUGE

20 sts and 24 rows = 4" in St st

PATTERN NOTES

Charts A, B, and C are on page 36. If you prefer to follow written instructions for the charted material, see "Written Instructions for Charts" on page 35.

If using stitch markers to mark each pattern repeat, on some rows the stitch markers will have to be rearranged. For chart B, the markers will move on rows 7, 9, 11, and 13. For chart C, the markers will move on rows 1, 5, 11, 13, 15, and 17. See page 6 for more information on how to move the markers.

INSTRUCTIONS

Begin shawl by working set-up rows as follows.

Work tab CO (page 76) as foll: CO 2 sts. Knit 18 rows. Turn work 90° and pick up 9 sts along the edge. Turn work 90° and pick up 2 sts from CO edge. (13 sts total)

Set-up row (WS): K2, P9, K2.

Inc row (RS): K2, (YO, K1) to last 2 sts, YO, K2. (23 sts)

Row 2: K2, purl to last 2 sts, K2.

Row 3: Knit all sts.

Row 4: Rep row 2.

Work inc row once more (43 sts). Work rows 2 and 3 another 3 times. Rep row 2 once more. Work inc row once more (83 sts). Rep rows 2 and 3 another 7 times. Rep row 2 once more. Work inc row once more (163 sts). Knit 2 rows.

Next row (RS): K2, PM, K51, PM, K1, PM, K55, PM, K1, PM, K51, PM, K2.

Next row (WS): K2, SM, K2, K1f&b, knit to next marker, SM, K1, SM, K2, K2tog, K25, K2tog, knit to 4 sts before next marker, K2tog, K2, SM, K1, SM, knit to 3 sts before next marker, K1f&b, K2, SM, K2. (162 sts)

Next row: Knit all sts.

Next row: K2, purl to last 2 sts, K2.

Body of Shawl

Cont working first 2 sts and last 2 sts in garter st (knit every row). Work spine sts (i.e., stitches with marker on either side) in St st (knit on RS, purl on WS). In between markers (starting with

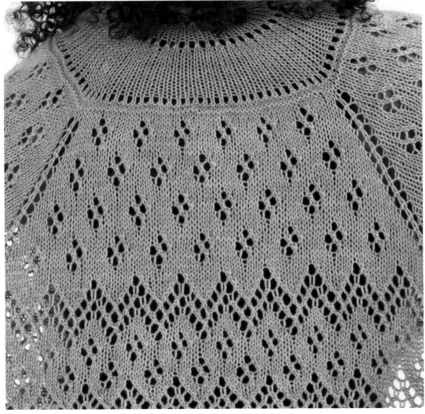

The lace transitions from a simple to a more complex pattern.

52 sts following set-up rows), work charts in following order:

Chart A 4 times. (258 sts)

Stitch Count	
First rep of chart A	186 sts
Second rep of chart A	210 sts
Third rep of chart A	234 sts
Fourth rep of chart A	258 sts

Chart B once. (306 sts)

Chart C once. (354 sts)

Chart B once. (402 sts)

Work rows 1–11 of chart C. (438 sts)

Make It Bigger!

Repeat charts B and C as desired, ending with chart B before moving on to final 11 rows of chart C. Make sure you have an extra skein of yarn!

FINISHING

BO loosely purlwise as described on page 78. With tapestry needle, weave in ends. Using blocking wires or pins, block to finished measurements.

WRITTEN INSTRUCTIONS FOR CHARTS

If you prefer to follow row-by-row written instructions rather than a chart, use the instructions below.

Chart A

Row 1 (RS): YO, K2, *K3, YO, ssk, K3; rep from * to 2 sts before marker, K2, YO.

Row 2 and all even-numbered rows (WS): Purl all sts.

Row 3: YO, K3, *K2, (YO, ssk) twice, K2; rep from * to 3 sts before marker, K3, YO.

Row 5: YO, K4, *K3, YO, ssk, K3; rep from * to 4 sts before marker, K4, YO.

Row 7: YO, knit to marker, YO.

Row 8: Purl all sts.

Rep rows 1–8 for patt.

Chart B

Row 1 (RS): YO, K2, *K3, YO, ssk, K3; rep from * to 2 sts before marker, K2, YO.

Row 2 and all even-numbered rows (WS): Purl all sts.

Row 3: YO, K3, *K1, K2tog, YO, K1, YO, ssk, K2; rep from * to 3 sts before marker, K3, YO.

Row 5: YO, K4, *(K2tog, YO) twice, K1, YO, ssk, K1; rep from * to 4 sts before marker, K4, YO.

Row 7: YO, K3, YO, sk2p, *YO, K2tog, YO, K1, YO, ssk, YO, sk2p; rep from * to 4 sts before marker, YO, K4, YO.

Row 9: YO, K3, YO, ssk, YO, *sk2p, YO, K3, YO, ssk, YO; rep from * to 7 sts before marker, sk2p, YO, K4, YO.

Row 11: YO, K5, YO, sk2p, *YO, K5, YO, sk2p; rep from * to 6 sts before marker, YO, K6, YO.

Row 13: YO, K2tog, K1, YO, ssk, K2, YO, *ssk, K2, YO; rep from * to 9 sts before marker, ssk, K2, YO, ssk, K1, ssk, YO.

Chart A (continued, column 3)

Row 15: YO, K2, (YO, ssk) twice, K2, *K2, (YO, ssk) twice, K2; rep from * to 8 sts before marker, K2, (YO, ssk) twice, K2, YO.

Row 17: YO, K4, YO, ssk, K3, *K3, YO, ssk, K3; rep from * to 9 sts before marker, K3, YO, ssk, K4, YO.

Row 18: Purl all sts.

Chart C

Row 1 (RS): YO, K1, YO, *ssk, K6, YO; rep from * to 3 sts before marker, ssk, K1, YO.

Row 2 and all even-numbered rows (WS): Purl all sts.

Row 3: YO, K1, YO, ssk, *YO, ssk, K4, YO, ssk; rep from * to last 3 sts before marker, YO, ssk, K1, YO.

Row 5: YO, K3, YO, *ssk, K2, YO; rep from * to last 5 sts before marker, ssk, K3, YO.

Row 7: YO, K1, YO, ssk, K2, *K1, K2tog, YO, K1, YO, ssk, K2; rep from * to last 5 sts before marker, K1, K2tog, YO, K2, YO.

Row 9: YO, K1, (YO, ssk) twice, K1, *K2tog, YO, K1, (YO, ssk) twice, K1; rep from * to last 6 sts before marker, (K2tog, YO) twice, K2, YO.

Row 11: YO, K3, YO, ssk, YO, sk2p, *YO, K2tog, YO, K1, YO, ssk, YO, sk2p; rep from * to last 6 sts before marker, YO, K2tog, YO, K4, YO.

Row 13: YO, K2tog, K3, YO, ssk, YO, *sk2p, YO, K3, YO, ssk, YO; rep from * to last 9 sts before marker, sk2p, YO, K4, ssk, YO.

Row 15: YO, K6, YO, sk2p, *YO, K5, YO, sk2p; rep from * to last 7 sts before marker, YO, K7, YO.

Row 17: YO, K8, YO, *ssk, K6, YO; rep from * to last 10 sts before marker, ssk, K8, YO.

Row 18: Purl all sts.

Sparrow Chart A

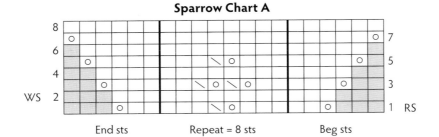

End sts   Repeat = 8 sts   Beg sts

Sparrow Chart B

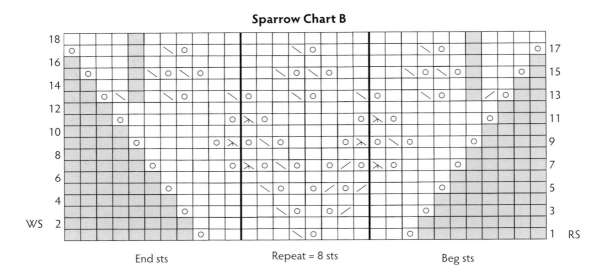

End sts   Repeat = 8 sts   Beg sts

Sparrow Chart C

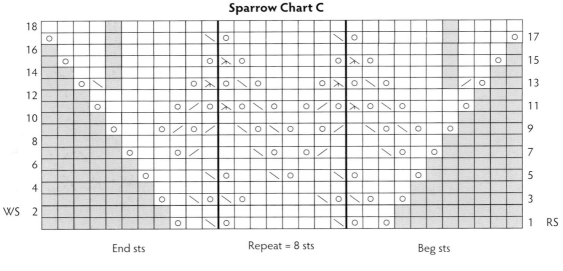

End sts   Repeat = 8 sts   Beg sts

Legend

☐ K on RS, P on WS	╱ K2tog
• P on RS, K on WS	⋊ Sk2p
╲ Ssk	▨ No stitch
⊙ YO	

STARLIT

This bottom-up short-row shawl features treelike lace at the edge that flows into the stockinette body. Try this shawl in a gradient yarn and it just might look like the northern lights bouncing off the night sky.

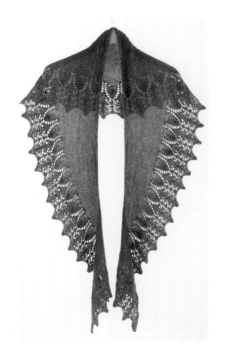

"Starlit," designed and knitted by author

Skill Level: Intermediate ◇ ◇ ◇ ◇
Finished Measurements: 17" x 78"

MATERIALS

1 skein of Muse from Twisted Fiber Art* (50% silk, 50% merino; 140 g; 660 yds) in color Phantom (Design: Evolution) **1**

US size 4 (3.5 mm) circular needle, 24" cable or longer, or size needed to obtain gauge

Tapestry needle

Blocking wires and/or blocking pins

* To order this yarn, purchase a double evolution—two 70g skeins—which will be dyed in one long color change over the total yardage.

GAUGE

16 sts and 36 rows = 4" in St st

PATTERN NOTES

Charts A and B are on page 40. If you prefer to follow written instructions for the charted material, see "Written Instructions for Charts" on page 39.

If using stitch markers to mark each pattern repeat, on some rows the stitch markers will have to be rearranged. For chart A, the markers will move on row 5. For chart B, the markers will be moved on rows 9, 11, 13, and 15. See page 6 for more information on how to move the markers.

INSTRUCTIONS

CO 435 sts. Work rows 1–6 of chart A 3 times. Work rows 1–16 of chart B. (349 sts)

Make It Bigger!

Have more yarn? Repeat chart A as many times as you like before moving on to chart B.

Row 1 (RS): K179, turn work. (170 sts unworked)

Row 2 (WS): P9, turn work. (170 sts unworked)

Row 3: K8, ssk, K4, turn work. (165 sts unworked; 348 sts total)

Row 4: P12, P2tog, P4, turn work. (165 sts unworked; 347 sts total)

Row 5: Knit to 1 st before gap (1 st before previous turning point), ssk, K4, turn work.

Row 6: Purl to 1 st before gap (1 st before previous turning point), P2tog, P4, turn work.

Work rows 5 and 6 another 32 times. (All sts have been worked; 281 sts rem)

Knit 4 rows.

FINISHING

BO loosely knitwise as described on page 77. With tapestry needle, weave in ends. Using blocking wires or pins, block to finished measurements.

WRITTEN INSTRUCTIONS FOR CHARTS

If you prefer to follow row-by-row written instructions rather than a chart, use the instructions below.

Chart A

Row 1 (RS): K2, K2tog, K3, YO, K1, *YO, K3, sk2p, K3, YO, K1; rep from * to last 7 sts, YO, K3, ssk, K2.

Rows 2 and 4 (WS): K2, purl to last 2 sts, K2.

Row 3: K2, K2tog, K2, YO, K2, *K1, YO, K2, sk2p, K2, YO, K2; rep from * to last 7 sts, K1, YO, K2, ssk, K2.

Row 5: K2, K2tog, (K1, YO) twice, sk2p, *(YO, K1) twice, sk2p, (K1, YO) twice, sk2p; rep from * to last 6 sts, (YO, K1) twice, ssk, K2.

Row 6: K2, purl to last 2 sts, K2.

Rep rows 1–6 for patt.

Chart B

Row 1 (RS): K2, *K3, K2tog, YO, K1, YO, ssk, K2; rep from * to last 3 sts, K3.

Row 2 and all even-numbered rows (WS): K2, purl to last 2 sts, K2.

Row 3: K2, *K2, K2tog, YO, K3, YO, ssk, K1; rep from * to last 3 sts, K3.

Row 5: K2, *K1, K2tog, YO, K5, YO, ssk; rep from * to last 3 sts, K3.

Row 7: K2, K2tog, YO, K4, *K3, YO, sk2p, YO, K4; rep from * to last 7 sts, K3, YO, ssk, K2.

Row 9: K2, *K1, YO, K3, sk2p, K3, YO; rep from * to last 3 sts, K3.

Rows 11 and 13: Rep row 9.

Row 15: K2, *K1, YO, ssk, K1, sk2p, K1, K2tog, YO; rep from * to last 3 sts, K3.

Row 16: K2, purl to last 2 sts, K2.

The gradient yarn adds extra dimension to the lace edge.

Starlit Chart A

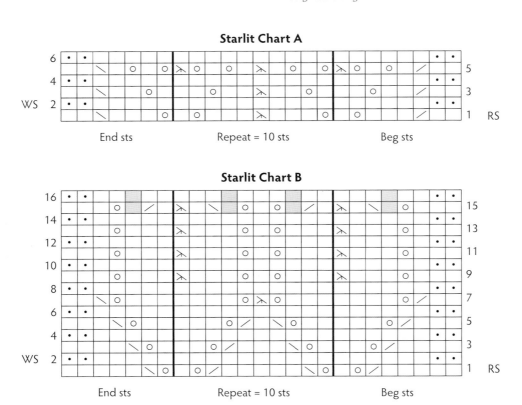

Legend

☐	K on RS, P on WS	⟋	K2tog
•	P on RS, K on WS	⟑	Sk2p
⟍	Ssk	☐	No stitch
○	YO		

EARTH AND SKY

If you liked the Briargate pattern in Sock-Yarn Shawls, *you'll love this shawl. With similar construction and style, it's another great addition to your wardrobe.*

"Earth and Sky," designed by author and knitted by Melissa Rusk

Skill Level: Experienced ◇ ◇ ◇ ◇
Finished Measurements: 21" x 80"

MATERIALS

Baby Boom Spirit of the Southwest from Fiesta Yarns (90% extra-fine superwash merino wool, 10% nylon; 4 oz; 440 yds) 〔**1**〕

A   1 skein in color Great Horned Owl
B   1 skein in color Rain Maker

US size 5 (3.75 mm) circular needle, 24" cable or longer, or size needed to obtain gauge

Tapestry needle

Blocking wires and/or blocking pins

GAUGE

20 sts and 32 rows = 4" in St st

PATTERN NOTES

The chart is on page 44. If you prefer to follow written instructions for the charted material, see "Written Instructions for Chart" on page 43.

If using stitch markers to mark each 8-stitch repeat in the chart, the stitch markers will need to be rearranged on row 5. See page 6 for more information on how to move the markers.

INSTRUCTIONS

With A, work tab CO (page 76) as foll: CO 3 sts. Knit 6 rows. Turn work 90° and pick up 3 sts along edge. Turn work 90° and pick up 3 sts from CO edge. (9 sts total)

Row 1 (RS): Cont with A, K2, (YO, K1) to last 2 sts, YO, K2. (15 sts)

Row 2 (WS): K3, YO, purl to last 3 sts, YO, K3. (17 sts)

Row 3: K2, YO, knit to last 2 sts, YO, K2. (19 sts)

Work rows 2 and 3 another 62 times. (267 sts)

Next row (WS): K3, YO, knit to last 3 sts, YO, K3. (269 sts)

Knit 2 rows.

Lace Edge

With B, work chart 3 times. (365 sts)

Stitch Count	
First rep of chart	301
Second rep of chart	333
Third rep of chart	365

With A, work final edging as follows:

Knit 2 rows.

Row 1 (RS): K2, YO, knit to last 2 sts, YO, K2. (367 sts)

Row 2 (WS): K3, YO, K2tog, knit to last 3 sts, YO, K3. (368 sts)

Row 3: K1, *YO twice, sk2p; rep from * to last st, YO twice, K1.

Row 4: K1, *(K1, P1) twice into double YO, K1; rep from * to last 3 sts, (K1, P1) twice into double YO, K1.

FINISHING

BO loosely knitwise as described on page 77. With tapestry needle, weave in ends. Using blocking wires or pins, block to finished measurements.

WRITTEN INSTRUCTIONS FOR CHART

If you prefer to follow row-by-row written instructions rather than a chart, use the instructions below.

Row 1 (RS): K2, YO, *K2, YO, ssk, K1, K2tog, YO, K1; rep from * to last 3 sts, K1, YO, K2.

Row 2 and all even-numbered rows (WS): K3, YO, purl to last 3 sts, YO, K3.

Row 3: K2, YO, K2, *K1, ssk, YO, K3, YO, K2tog; rep from * to last 5 sts, K3, YO, K2.

Row 5: K2, YO, K1, YO, K2, YO, *sk2p, YO, K2tog, YO, K1, YO, ssk, YO; rep from * to last 8 sts, sk2p, YO, K2, YO, K1, YO, K2.

Row 7: (K2, YO) twice, K3, YO, ssk, *K1, K2tog, YO, K3, YO, ssk; rep from * to last 10 sts, K1, K2tog, YO, K3, (YO, K2) twice.

Row 9: K2, (YO, K1) twice, *K2, YO, K2tog, K1, ssk, YO, K1; rep from * to last 5 sts, K2, YO, K1, YO, K2.

Row 11: K2, YO, K3, YO, K2tog, YO, *K1, YO, ssk, YO, sk2p, YO, K2tog, YO; rep from * to last 8 sts, K1, YO, ssk, YO, K3, YO, K2.

Row 12: K3, YO, purl to last 3 sts, YO, K3.

Rep rows 1–12 for patt.

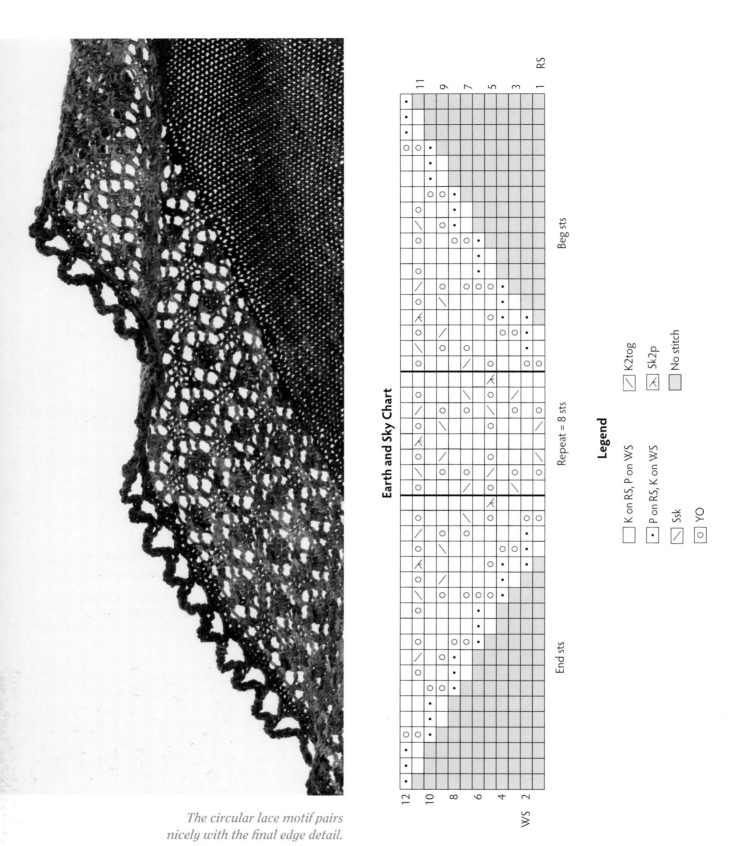

The circular lace motif pairs nicely with the final edge detail.

Earth and Sky Chart

Legend

	K on RS, P on WS		K2tog
•	P on RS, K on WS		Sk2p
/	Ssk		No stitch
○	YO		

SIERRA

Sometimes a lace pattern is so beautiful on its own that it doesn't need to be complicated with elaborate shawl shaping. Sierra is a simple lace stole where the peaks and valleys in the lace are the true star.

"Sierra," designed by author and knitted by Cathy Rusk

Skill Level: Easy ◇ ◇ ◇ ◇
Finished Measurements: 13" x 70"

MATERIALS

1 skein of Muse from Twisted Fiber Art* (50% silk, 50% merino; 140 g; 660 yds) in color Dazzle (Design: Evolution) **1**

US size 5 (3.75 mm) circular needle, 24" cable or longer, or size needed to obtain gauge

Tapestry needle

Blocking wires and/or blocking pins

* To order this yarn, purchase a double evolution—two 70g skeins—which will be dyed in one long color change over the total yardage.

GAUGE

20 sts and 32 rows = 4" in St st

PATTERN NOTES

The chart is on page 47. If you prefer to follow written instructions for the charted material, see "Written Instructions for Chart" on page 47.

If using stitch markers to mark each pattern repeat, the stitch markers will have to be rearranged on row 17. See page 6 for more information on how to move the markers.

INSTRUCTIONS

CO 66 sts. Knit 1 row.

Work chart until piece measures 60" or desired length, ending with row 21 of chart.

Last row (WS): Knit all sts.

Make It Bigger!

For a wider piece, add a multiple of 12 stitches to the cast on and work the lace repeat additional times. The stole can be knit as long as you like, just end with row 21 of the lace chart before working the last row.

FINISHING

BO loosely knitwise as described on page 77. With tapestry needle, weave in ends. Using blocking wires or pins, block to finished measurements.

WRITTEN INSTRUCTIONS FOR CHART

If you prefer to follow row-by-row written instructions rather than a chart, use the instructions below.

Row 1 (RS): K3, (K2tog, YO) to last 3 sts, K3.

Row 2 and all even-numbered rows (WS): K2, purl to last 2 sts, K2.

Row 3: K3, *(YO, K2tog) 3 times, K2, (YO, K2tog) twice; rep from * to last 3 sts, K3.

Row 5: K3, *(K2tog, YO) twice, K2tog, K4, YO, K2tog, YO; rep from * to last 3 sts, K3.

Row 7: K3, *(YO, K2tog) twice, K2, YO, ssk, K2, YO, K2tog; rep from * to last 3 sts, K3.

Row 9: K3, *K2tog, YO, K2tog, K1, K2tog, YO, K1, YO, ssk, K2, YO; rep from * to last 3 sts, K3.

Row 11: K3, *YO, K2tog, K1, K2tog, YO, K3, YO, ssk, K2; rep from * to last 3 sts, K3.

Row 13: K3, *K2, K2tog, YO, K2, YO, K2tog, K1, YO, ssk, K1; rep from * to last 3 sts, K3.

Row 15: K3, *K1, K2tog, YO, K2, (YO, K2tog) twice, K1, YO, ssk; rep from * to last 3 sts, K3.

Row 17: K2, YO, *sk2p, YO, K2, (YO, K2tog) 3 times, K1, YO; rep from * to last 4 sts, ssk, K2.

Row 19: K3, *YO, K2tog, K1, (YO, K2tog) 4 times, K1; rep from * to last 3 sts, K3.

Row 21: K3, *K2, (YO, K2tog) 5 times; rep from * to last 3 sts, K3.

Row 22: K2, purl to last 2 sts, K2.

Rep rows 1–22 for patt.

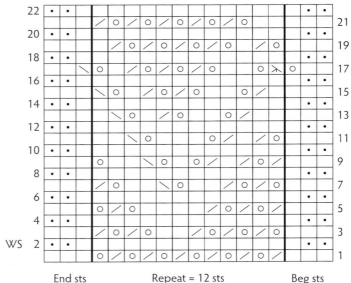

Sierra Chart

WS ... RS

End sts   Repeat = 12 sts   Beg sts

Legend

☐ K on RS, P on WS	◦ YO	╲ Ssk
• P on RS, K on WS	⋋ Sk2p	╱ K2tog

FLOE

Here's another short-row shawl with a twist. The border is worked sideways, with stitches for the body of the shawl being added along the side of the border as you go with wrap and turns—a fun new way to work a lace border!

"Floe," designed by author and knitted by Melissa Rusk

Skill Level: Experienced ◇ ◇ ◇ ◇
Finished Measurements: 15" x 68"

MATERIALS

Caper Sock from String Theory Hand Dyed Yarn (80% superwash merino wool, 10% cashmere, 10% nylon; 113 g; 400 yds) (**1**)

  A 1 skein in color Brina
  B 1 skein in color Agave

US size 4 (3.5 mm) circular needle, 24" cable or longer, or size needed to obtain gauge

1 stitch marker

Tapestry needle

Blocking wires and/or blocking pins

GAUGE

16 sts and 36 rows = 4" in St st

SPECIAL ABBREVIATIONS

W&t: Move yarn to front, slip next st purlwise to RH needle, move yarn to back, move st back to LH needle, turn.

PATTERN NOTES

The chart is on page 51. If you prefer to follow written instructions for the charted material, see "Written Instructions for Chart" on page 50.

When working rows 5 and 6 of the lace border section, you are working the next row of the chart with each repeat. This means you are repeating the chart while at the same time working the instructions given in rows 5 and 6.

INSTRUCTIONS

Begin shawl by working lace border as follows.

Lace Border

With A, CO 23 sts.

Row 1 (RS): K1f&b, PM, knit to end. (24 sts)

Row 2 (WS): Knit to marker, SM, K1, w&t, turn work.

Row 3: K1f&b, SM, work row 1 of chart to end.

Row 4: Work row 2 of chart to marker, SM, K1, w&t, turn work, leaving rem sts unworked.

Row 5: K1f&b, SM, work next row of chart to end.

Row 6: Work next row of chart to marker, SM, K1, w&t, turn work leaving rem sts unworked.

Rep last 2 rows until chart is repeated 17 times total, ending with row 36 of chart. (330 sts, 22 sts on one side of stitch marker, 308 sts on the other)

Next row (RS): K1, SM, knit to end. BO 23 sts on WS, removing marker. (307 sts rem)

Short-Row Body

Set-up row (WS): With A, K2, K2tog, knit to last 4 sts, K2tog, K2. (305 sts)

Cut A. Use B for remainder of shawl.

Row 1 (RS): K157, turn work.

Row 2 (WS): P9, turn work.

Row 3: K8, ssk, K3, turn work. (304 sts)

Row 4: P11, P2tog, P3, turn work. (303 sts)

Row 5: Knit to 1 st before gap (1 st before previous turning point), ssk, K3, turn work.

Row 6: Purl to 1 st before gap (1 st before previous turning point), P2tog, P3.

Work rows 5 and 6 another 35 times (231 sts). All sts have been worked. Knit 6 rows.

FINISHING

BO loosely knitwise as described on page 77. With tapestry needle, weave in ends. Using blocking wires or pins, block to finished measurements.

WRITTEN INSTRUCTIONS FOR CHART

If you prefer to follow row-by-row written instructions rather than a chart, use the following instructions.

Row 1 (RS): K2, YO, K2, ssk, K4, K2tog, K2, YO, K1, (YO, ssk) twice, YO, K3.

Row 2 (WS): K2, P21.

Row 3: K3, YO, K2, ssk, K2, K2tog, K2, YO, K3, (YO, ssk) twice, YO, K3.

Row 4: K2, P22.

Row 5: K2, YO, ssk, YO, K2, ssk, K2tog, K2, YO, K5, (YO, ssk) twice, YO, K3.

Row 6: K2, P23.

Row 7: K3, YO, ssk, YO, K2, ssk, K4, K2tog, K2, YO, K1, (YO, ssk) twice, YO, K3.

Row 8: K2, P24.

Row 9: K2, (YO, ssk) twice, YO, K2, ssk, K2, K2tog, K2, YO, K3, (YO, ssk) twice, YO, K3.

Row 10: K2, P25.

Row 11: K3, (YO, ssk) twice, YO, K2, ssk, K2tog, K2, YO, K5, (YO, ssk) twice, YO, K3.

Row 12: K2, P26.

Row 13: K4, (YO, ssk) twice, YO, K2, ssk, K4, K2tog, K2, YO, K1, (YO, ssk) twice, YO, K3.

Row 14: K2, P27.

Row 15: K3, (YO, ssk) 3 times, YO, K2, ssk, K2, K2tog, K2, YO, K3, (YO, ssk) twice, YO, K3.

Row 16: K2, P28.

Row 17: K4, (YO, ssk) 3 times, YO, K2, ssk, K2tog, K2, YO, K5, (YO, ssk) twice, YO, K3.

Row 18: K2, P29.

Row 19: K2tog, K2, YO, (K2tog, YO) 3 times, K1, YO, K2, ssk, K4, K2tog, K2, (YO, K2tog) 3 times, K2.

Row 20: K2, P28.

Row 21: K3, (K2tog, YO) 3 times, K3, YO, K2, ssk, K2, K2tog, K2, (YO, K2tog) 3 times, K2.

Row 22: K2, P27.

Row 23: K2, (K2tog, YO) 3 times, K5, YO, K2, ssk, K2tog, K2, (YO, K2tog) 3 times, K2.

Row 24: K2, P26.

Row 25: K1, (K2tog, YO) 3 times, K1, YO, K2, ssk, K4, K2tog, K2, (YO, K2tog) 3 times, K2.

Row 26: K2, P25.

Row 27: K2, (K2tog, YO) twice, K3, YO, K2, ssk, K2, K2tog, K2, (YO, K2tog) 3 times, K2.

Row 28: K2, P24.

Row 29: K1, (K2tog, YO) twice, K5, YO, K2, ssk, K2tog, K2, (YO, K2tog) 3 times, K2.

Row 30: K2, P23.

Row 31: K2, K2tog, YO, K1, YO, K2, ssk, K4, K2tog, K2, (YO, K2tog) 3 times, K2.

Row 32: K2, P22.

Row 33: K1, K2tog, YO, K3, YO, K2, ssk, K2, K2tog, K2, (YO, K2tog) 3 times, K2.

Row 34: K2, P21.

Row 35: K7, YO, K2, ssk, K2tog, K2, (YO, K2tog) 3 times, K2.

Row 36: K2, P20.

Rep rows 1–36 for patt.

Floe Chart

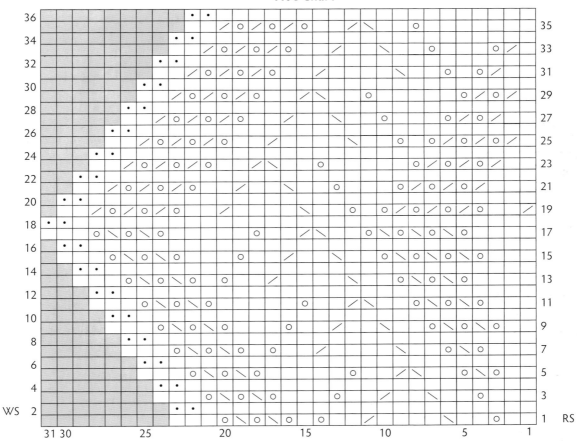

Legend

☐ K on RS, P on WS	⊙ YO
• P on RS, K on WS	╱ K2tog
╲ Ssk	▨ No stitch

DEMETER

Half-pi (semicircle) shawls are perfect for someone wanting a cozy shawl. The shape allows for excellent drape, hanging on your shoulders like a cape. Simple lace patterns and easy increases make this pattern an excellent choice if you're trying this shawl shape for the first time.

"Demeter," designed by author and knitted by Jenni Lesniak

Skill Level: Intermediate ◇ ◇ ◇ ◇
Finished Measurements: 29" x 54"

MATERIALS

2 skeins of Breathless from Shalimar Yarns (75% superwash merino, 15% cashmere, 10% silk; 100 g; 420 yds) in color Limerick **1**

US size 4 (3.5 mm) circular needle, 24" cable or longer, or size needed to obtain gauge

Tapestry needle

Blocking wires and/or blocking pins

GAUGE

24 sts and 28 rows = 4" in St st

PATTERN NOTES

Charts A, B, C, and D are on page 55. If you prefer to follow written instructions for the charted material, see "Written Instructions for Charts" on page 54.

If using stitch markers to mark each pattern repeat, on some rows the stitch markers will have to be rearranged. For chart B, the markers will move on row 7. For chart C, the markers will move on rows 1 and 3. For chart D, the markers will be moved on row 1. See page 6 for more information on how to move the markers.

INSTRUCTIONS

After the set-up rows, this shawl is worked in 5 different stitch-pattern sections.

Set-Up Rows

Work tab CO (page 76) as foll: CO 3 sts. Knit 6 rows. Turn work 90° and pick up 3 sts along edge. Turn work 90° and pick up 3 sts from CO edge (9 sts total). Knit 1 row.

Section 1

4 rows

Inc row (RS): (K1, YO) to last st, K1. (17 sts)

Knit 3 rows.

Section 2

8 rows

Inc row (RS): (K1, YO) to last st, K1. (33 sts)

Row 2 (WS): K2, purl to last 2 sts, K2.

Row 3: Knit all sts.

Work rows 2 and 3 twice more. Rep row 2 once more.

Section 3

18 rows

Inc row (RS): (K1, YO) to last st, K1. (65 sts)

Next row (WS): K2, YO, purl to last 2 sts, YO, K2. (67 sts)

Work chart A 4 times (16 rows).

Section 4

34 rows

Inc row (RS): (K1, YO) to last st, K1. (133 sts)

Next row (RS): K2, purl to last 2 sts, K2.

Work chart B 4 times (32 rows).

Section 5

109 rows

Inc row (RS): (K1, YO) to last st, K1. (265 sts)

Next row (RS): K2, purl to last 2 sts, K2.

Work chart C 4 times (48 rows).

Work chart D 14 times (56 rows). Work rows 1–3 of chart D once more.

Make It Bigger!

With extra yarn, you can repeat chart C an extra time, or repeat chart D as many times as desired.

FINISHING

BO loosely purlwise as described on page 78. With tapestry needle, weave in ends. Using blocking wires or pins, block to finished measurements.

WRITTEN INSTRUCTIONS FOR CHARTS

If you prefer to follow row-by-row written instructions rather than a chart, use the instructions below.

Chart A

Row 1 (RS): K4, K2tog, YO, *K1, YO, ssk, K1, K2tog, YO; rep from * to last 7 sts, K1, YO, ssk, K4.

Rows 2 and 4 (WS): K2, purl to last 2 sts, K2.

Row 3: K3, K2tog, YO, K1, *K2, YO, sk2p, YO, K1; rep from * to last 7 sts, K2, YO, ssk, K3.

Rep rows 1–4 for patt.

Chart B

Row 1 (RS): K4, K2tog, YO, *K1, YO, ssk, K1, K2tog, YO; rep from * to last 7 sts, K1, YO, ssk, K4.

Row 2 and all even-numbered rows (WS): K2, purl to last 2 sts, K2.

Row 3: K3, K2tog, K1, YO, *K1, YO, K1, sk2p, K1, YO; rep from * to last 7 sts, K1, YO, K1, ssk, K3.

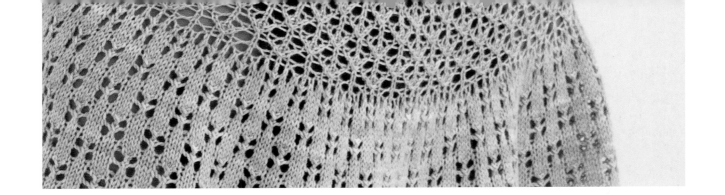

Row 5: K4, YO, ssk, *K1, K2tog, YO, K1, YO, ssk; rep from * to last 7 sts, K1, K2tog, YO, K4.

Row 7: K4, YO, K1, *sk2p, (K1, YO) twice, K1; rep from * to last 8 sts, sk2p, K1, YO, K4.

Row 8: K2, purl to last 2 sts, K2.

Rep rows 1–8 for patt.

Chart C

Row 1 (RS): K2, *K3, YO, sk2p, YO; rep from * to last 5 sts, K5.

Row 2 and all even-numbered rows (WS): K2, purl to last 2 sts, K2.

Row 3: Rep row 1.

Row 5: Knit all sts.

Row 7: K2, *YO, sk2p, YO, K3; rep from * to last 5 sts, YO, sk2p, YO, K2.

Row 9: Rep row 7.

Row 11: Knit all sts.

Row 12: K2, purl to last 2 sts, K2.

Rep rows 1–12 for patt.

Chart D

Row 1 (RS): K2, *K3, YO, sk2p, YO; rep from * to last 5 sts, K5.

Rows 2 and 4 (WS): K2, purl to last 2 sts, K2.

Row 3: K2, *YO, sk2p, YO, K3; rep from * to last 5 sts, YO, sk2p, YO, K2.

Rep rows 1–4 for patt.

Demeter Chart A

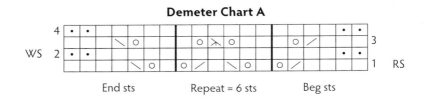

Demeter Chart B

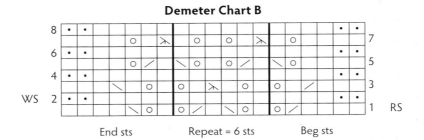

Demeter Chart C

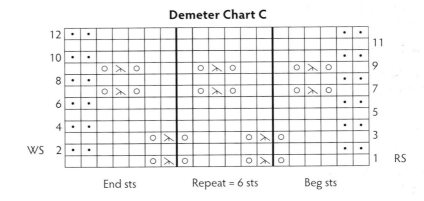

Demeter Chart D

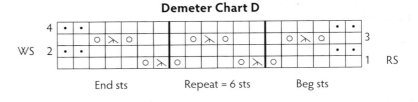

Legend

☐ K on RS, P on WS	◦ YO
• P on RS, K on WS	╱ K2tog
╲ Ssk	⋋ Sk2p

LYCOPOD

A delicate top-down triangle shawl, Lycopod is the perfect warm-weather piece. It can easily be made larger or smaller, depending on the knitter's mood.

"Lycopod," designed by author and knitted by Beth Klein

Skill Level: Intermediate ◇ ◇ ◇ ◇
Finished Measurements: 41" x 84"

MATERIALS

2 skeins of Tosh Sock from Madelintosh (100% superwash merino wool; 100 g; 395 yds) in color Cousteau **1**
US size 4 (3.5 mm) circular needle, 24" cable or longer, or size needed to obtain gauge
4 stitch markers
Tapestry needle
Blocking wires and/or blocking pins

GAUGE

20 sts and 24 rows = 4" in St st

PATTERN NOTES

Charts A, B, and C are on page 60. If you prefer to follow written instructions for the charted material, see "Written Instructions for Charts" on page 58.

Charts for this pattern show RS rows only. See "Instructions," on page 58 for how to work WS rows.

If using stitch markers to mark each pattern repeat, on some rows the stitch markers will have to be rearranged. For chart B, the markers will move on rows 5, 9, and 13. For chart C, the markers will move on rows 9, 11, 13, 19, and 21. See page 6 for more information on how to move the markers.

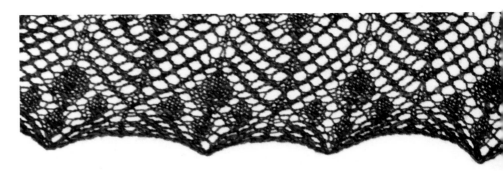

INSTRUCTIONS

Begin shawl by working set-up rows as follows.

Work tab CO (page 76) as foll: CO 3 sts. Knit 6 rows. Turn work 90° and pick up 3 sts along the edge. Turn work 90° and pick up 3 sts from CO edge. (9 sts total)

Set-up row (WS): K3, PM, P1, PM, P1 (center st), PM, P1, PM, K3.

Body of Shawl

Row 1 (RS): K3, SM, work row 1 of chart A, SM, K1, SM, work row 1 of chart A, SM, K3.

Row 2 and all even-numbered rows: K3, purl to last 3 sts slipping the markers along the way, K3.

Cont working first 3 sts and last 3 sts in garter st (knit every row) and the center st in St st (knit on RS, purl on WS). On all WS rows, work row 2 of body of shawl (above). Work charts on each half of shawl as foll:

Chart A (41 sts)

Chart B (105 sts)

Chart C (169 sts)

Chart B (233 sts)

Chart C (297 sts)

Chart B (361 sts)

Chart C (425 sts)

Do not work final WS row.

FINISHING

BO loosely purlwise as described on page 78. With tapestry needle, weave in ends. Using blocking wires or pins, block to finished measurements.

Make It Bigger (or Smaller)!

With extra yarn, you can add as many repeats of charts B and C as you like. If you want a smaller shawl, work fewer repeats of charts B and C.

WRITTEN INSTRUCTIONS FOR CHARTS

If you prefer to follow row-by-row written instructions rather than a chart, use the instructions below.

Chart A

Row 1 (RS): YO, K1, YO.

Row 3: YO, K3, YO.

Row 5: YO, K5, YO.

Row 7: YO, K2, YO, sk2p, YO, K2, YO.

Row 9: YO, K2, K2tog, YO, K1, YO, ssk, K2, YO.

Row 11: YO, K2, K2tog, YO, K3, YO, ssk, K2, YO.

Row 13: YO, K2, (K2tog, YO) twice, K1, (YO, ssk) twice, K2, YO.

Row 15: YO, K2, (K2tog, YO) twice, K3, (YO, ssk) twice, K2, YO.

Chart B

Row 1 (RS): YO, K1, *K1, (K2tog, YO) 3 times, K1, (YO, ssk) 3 times, K2; rep from * to marker, YO.

Row 3: YO, K2, *(K2tog, YO) 3 times, K3, (YO, ssk) 3 times, K1; rep from * to last st before marker, K1, YO.

Row 5: YO, K1, YO, sk2p, *YO, (K2tog, YO) twice, K5, (YO, ssk) twice, YO, sk2p; rep from * to last st before marker, YO, K1, YO.

Row 7: YO, K4, *(K2tog, YO) twice, K7, (YO, ssk) twice, K1; rep from * to 3 sts before marker, K3, YO.

Row 9: YO, K1, YO, ssk, YO, sk2p, *YO, K2tog, YO, K1, YO, K2, sk2p, K2, YO, K1, YO, ssk, YO, sk2p; rep from * to last 3 sts before marker, YO, K2tog, YO, K1, YO.

Row 11: YO, K6, *K2tog, YO, K3, YO, K1, sk2p, K1, YO, K3, YO, ssk, K1; rep from * to last 5 sts before marker, K5, YO.

Row 13: *YO, K5, YO, sk2p; rep from * to last 5 sts before marker, YO, K5, YO.

Row 15: YO, K8, *K1, YO, K1, sk2p, K1, YO, K3, YO, K1, sk2p, K1, YO, K2; rep from * to last 7 sts before marker, K7, YO.

Row 17: YO, K2, YO, K4, K2tog, YO, K1, *YO, ssk, YO, sk2p, YO, K5, YO, sk2p, YO, K2tog, YO, K1; rep from * to last 8 sts before marker, YO, ssk, K4, YO, K2, YO.

Row 19: YO, (K1, YO) twice, ssk, K3, K2tog, YO, K2, *K1, (YO, ssk) twice, YO, K1, sk2p, K1, YO, (K2tog, YO) twice, K2; rep from * to last 10 sts before marker, K1, YO, ssk, K3, K2tog, (YO, K1) twice, YO.

Row 21: YO, K2, YO, K1, (YO, ssk) twice, K1, (K2tog, YO) twice, K1, *(YO, ssk) 3 times, YO, sk2p, YO, (K2tog, YO) 3 times, K1; rep from * to last 12 sts before marker, (YO, ssk) twice, K1, (K2tog, YO) twice, K1, YO, K2, YO.

Row 23: YO, K1, YO, K2tog, YO, K3, YO, ssk, YO, sk2p, YO, K2tog, YO, K2, *K1, (YO, ssk) 3 times, K1,

(K2tog, YO) 3 times, K2; rep from * to last 14 sts before marker, K1, YO, ssk, YO, sk2p, YO, K2tog, YO, K3, YO, ssk, YO, K1, YO.

Chart C

Row 1 (RS): YO, K1, *(YO, ssk) 3 times, YO, sk2p, YO, (K2tog, YO) 3 times, K1; rep from * to marker, YO.

Row 3: YO, K2, *K1, (YO, ssk) 3 times, K1, (K2tog, YO) 3 times, K2; rep from * to last st before marker, K1, YO.

Row 5: YO, K3, *K2, (YO, ssk) twice, YO, sk2p, YO, (K2tog, YO) twice, K3; rep from * to last 2 sts before marker, K2, YO.

Row 7: YO, K4, *K3, (YO, ssk) twice, K1, (K2tog, YO) twice, K4; rep from * to last 3 sts before marker, K3, YO.

Row 9: YO, K1, YO, K2, sk2p, *K2, YO, K1, YO, ssk, YO, sk2p, YO, K2tog, YO, K1, YO, K2, sk2p; rep from * to last 3 sts before marker, K2, YO, K1, YO.

Row 11: YO, K3, YO, K1, sk2p, *K1, YO, K3, YO, ssk, K1, K2tog, YO, K3, YO, K1, sk2p; rep from * to last 4 sts before marker, K1, YO, K3, YO.

Row 13: *YO, K5, YO, sk2p; rep from * to last 5 sts before marker, YO, K5, YO.

Row 15: YO, K8, *K1, YO, K1, sk2p, K1, YO, K3, YO, K1, sk2p, K1, YO, K2; rep from * to 7 sts before marker, K7, YO.

Row 17: YO, K2, YO, K7, *K2, YO, sk2p, YO, K2tog, YO, K1, YO, ssk, YO, sk2p, YO, K3; rep from * to last 8 sts before marker, K6, YO, K2, YO.

Row 19: YO, K1, YO, K3, (YO, ssk) twice, YO, K1, sk2p, *K1, YO, (K2tog, YO) twice, K3, (YO, ssk) twice, YO, K1, sk2p; rep from * to last 9 sts before marker, K1, YO, (K2tog, YO) twice, K3, YO, K1, YO.

Row 21: YO, K2, YO, K3, (YO, ssk) 3 times, YO, sk2p, *YO, (K2tog, YO) 3 times, K1, (YO, ssk) 3 times, YO, sk2p; rep from * to last 11 sts before marker, YO, (K2tog, YO) 3 times, K3, YO, K2, YO.

Row 23: YO, K1, YO, K2tog, YO, K5, (YO, ssk) 3 times, K1, *(K2tog, YO) 3 times, K3, (YO, ssk) 3 times, K1; rep from * to last 14 sts before marker, (K2tog, YO) 3 times, K5, YO, ssk, YO, K1, YO.

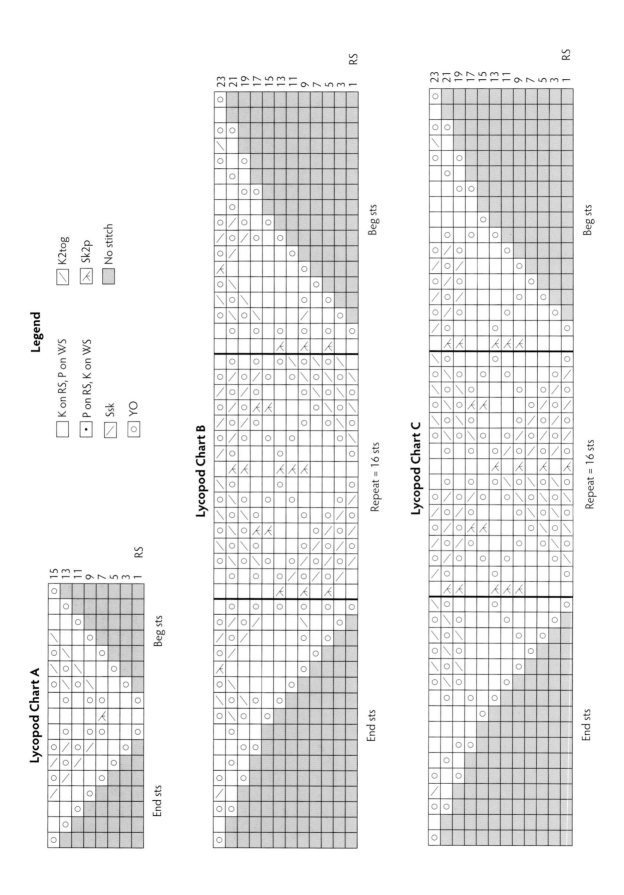

Legend

☐ K on RS, P on WS	☐ K2tog
• P on RS, K on WS	⅄ Sk2p
╱ Ssk	▦ No stitch
○ YO	

Lycopod Chart A

Lycopod Chart B

Repeat = 16 sts

Lycopod Chart C

Repeat = 16 sts

Large Shawls

Make any of these showstopping large shawls to show off your lace knitting skills and keep you cozy and warm! The projects in this section need 900 yards or more of sock yarn.

HARVEST

If you're ready for a challenge, this shawl is for you. Cables, lace, and a join-as-you-go border—this shawl has it all! Its half-pi (semicircle) shape and cozy cables make it the perfect cool-weather accessory.

"Harvest," designed by author and knitted by Jenni Lesniak

Skill Level: Experienced ◇ ◇ ◇ ◇
Finished Measurements: 38" x 78"

MATERIALS

3 skeins of Divine from Hazel Knits (75% superwash merino, 15% cashmere, 10% silk; 115 g; 400 yds) in color Hoppy Blonde **1**

US size 5 (3.75 mm) circular needle, 32" cable or longer, or size needed to obtain gauge

Cable needle

Tapestry needle

Blocking wires and/or blocking pins

GAUGE

22 sts and 32 rows = 4" in St st

SPECIAL ABBREVIATIONS

2/2CB: Sl 2 sts to cn and hold at back, K2, K2 from cn.

1/2CF: Sl 1 st to cn and hold at front, K2, K1 from cn.

2/1CB: Sl 2 sts to cn and hold at back, K1, K2 from cn.

2/2CF: Sl 2 sts to cn and hold at front, K2, K2 from cn.

PATTERN NOTES

For chart D, the final ssk on RS rows is completed by using 1 stitch from the border and 1 stitch from the body of the shawl.

Charts A, B, C, and D are on page 66. If you prefer to follow written instructions for the charted material, see "Written Instructions for Charts" on page 65.

INSTRUCTIONS

Begin shawl by working set-up rows as follows.

Work tab CO (page 76) as foll: CO 3 sts. Knit 6 rows. Turn work 90° and pick up 3 sts along the edge. Turn work 90° and pick up 3 sts from CO edge. (9 sts total)

Row 1 (RS): Knit all sts.

Row 2 (WS): K3, (YO, P1) 3 times, YO, K3. (13 sts)

Row 3: (K3, YO) twice, K1, (YO, K3) twice. (17 sts)

Row 4 and all even-numbered rows: K3, purl to last 3 sts, K3.

Row 5: K3, (YO, K1) 11 times, YO, K3. (29 sts)

Row 7: Knit all sts.

Row 9: K3, (YO, K1) to last 3 sts, YO, K3. (53 sts)

Row 11: K3, (YO, K2tog) to last 4 sts, YO, K4. (54 sts)

Row 13: K4, (YO, K2tog) to last 4 sts, YO, K1, YO, K3. (56 sts)

Row 15: K3, (YO, K2tog) to last 3 sts, YO, K3. (57 sts)

Row 16: K3, purl to last 3 sts, K3.

Body of Shawl

Inc row (RS): K3, (YO, K1) to last 3 sts, YO, K3. (109 sts)

Next row (WS): K3, purl to last 3 sts, K3.

Work chart A 4 times (24 rows).

Inc row (RS): K3, (YO, K1) to last 3 sts, YO, K3. (213 sts)

Next row (WS): K3, purl to last 3 sts, K3.

Work chart B 6 times (48 rows).

Inc row (RS): K3, (YO, K1) to last 3 sts, YO, K3. (421 sts)

Next row (WS): K3, purl to last 3 sts, K3.

Work chart C 5 times (60 rows). Work rows 1–11 of chart C once more.

Next row (WS): K2, K1f&b, knit to end. (422 sts)

Lace Edge

Using knitted cast on (page 76), CO 21 sts.

Row 1 (RS): K21, ssk with 1 st from body of shawl.

Row 2 (WS): Sl 1 wyib, knit to end.

Work chart D 140 times. Work rows 1 and 2 once more.

FINISHING

BO loosely knitwise as described on page 77. With tapestry needle, weave in ends. Using blocking wires or pins, block to finished measurements.

WRITTEN INSTRUCTIONS FOR CHARTS

If you prefer to follow row-by-row written instructions rather than a chart, use the instructions below.

Chart A

Row 1 (RS): K4, *P1, K4, K3tog, YO, K1, YO, P2, K4, P2, YO, K1, YO, sssk, K4; rep from * to last 5 sts, P1, K4.

Rows 2 and 4 (WS): K3, P1, K1, *P8, K2, P4, K2, P8, K1; rep from * to last 4 sts, P1, K3.

Row 3: K4, *P1, K2, K3tog, (K1, YO) twice, K1, P2, K4, P2, (K1, YO) twice, K1, sssk, K2; rep from * to last 5 sts, P1, K4.

Row 5: K4, *P1, K3tog, K2, YO, K1, YO, K2, P2, 2/2CB, P2, K2, YO, K1, YO, K2, sssk; rep from * to last 5 sts, P1, K4.

Row 6: K3, P1, K1, *P8, K2, P4, K2, P8, K1; rep from * to last 4 sts, P1, K3.

Rep rows 1–6 for patt.

Chart B

Row 1 (RS): K6, *K1, YO, K2, ssk, K3; rep from * to last 7 sts, K7.

Row 2 and all even-numbered rows (WS): K3, purl to last 3 sts, K3.

Row 3: K6, *K2, YO, K2, ssk, K2; rep from * to last 7 sts, K7.

Row 5: K6, *YO, K5, K2tog, K1; rep from * to last 7 sts, YO, K2, K2tog, K3.

Row 7: K3, K2tog, K1, YO, *K5, K2tog, YO, K1; rep from * to last 7 sts, K7.

Row 8: K3, purl to last 3 sts, K3.

Rep rows 1–8 for patt.

Chart C

Row 1 (RS): K3, 1/2CF, *K1, 2/1CB, K1, 1/2CF; rep from * to last 7 sts, K1, 2/1CB, K3.

Row 2 and all even-numbered rows (WS): K3, purl to last 3 sts, K3.

Row 3: K6, *YO, K2tog, K6; rep from * to last 7 sts, YO, K2tog, K5.

Row 5: K4, ssk, YO, *K6, ssk, YO; rep from * to last 7 sts, K7.

Row 7: K3, 2/1CB, *K1, 1/2CF, K1, 2/1CB; rep from * to last 7 sts, K1, 1/2CF, K3.

Row 9: K6, *K4, YO, K2tog, K2; rep from * to last 7 sts, K7.

Row 11: K6, *K2, ssk, YO, K4; rep from * to last 7 sts, K2, ssk, YO, K3.

Row 12: K3, purl to last 3 sts, K3.

Rep rows 1–12 for patt.

Chart D

Row 1 (RS): K3, (YO, K2tog) twice, K8, (YO, K2tog) twice, K1, ssk 1 st of border with 1 st of body of shawl.

Rows 2 and 4 (WS): Sl 1 wyib, P1, (YO, P2tog) twice, P8, (YO, P2tog) twice, P1, K2.

Row 3: Rep row 1.

Row 5: K3, (YO, K2tog) twice, 2/2CB, 2/2CF, (YO, K2tog) twice, K1, ssk 1 st of border with 1 st of body of shawl.

Row 6: Sl 1 wyib, P1, (YO, P2tog) twice, P8, (YO, P2tog) twice, P1, K2.

Rep rows 1–6 for patt.

Harvest Chart A

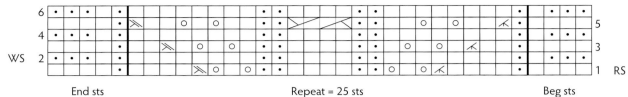

End sts Repeat = 25 sts Beg sts

Harvest Chart B

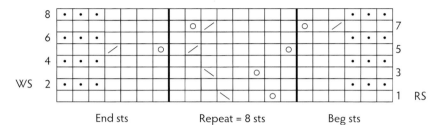

End sts Repeat = 8 sts Beg sts

Harvest Chart C

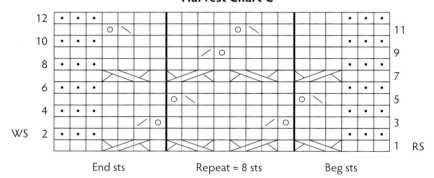

End sts Repeat = 8 sts Beg sts

Harvest Chart D

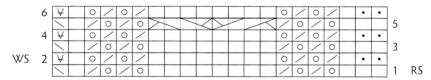

Repeat = 21 sts

Legend

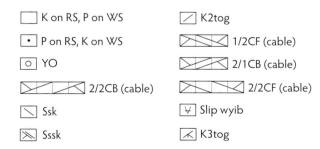

☐ K on RS, P on WS	╱ K2tog
• P on RS, K on WS	1/2CF (cable)
○ YO	2/1CB (cable)
2/2CB (cable)	2/2CF (cable)
╲ Ssk	¥ Slip wyib
Sssk	K3tog

DAYLILY

Leaf motifs and feather and fan come together to make this stunning circular pi shawl. This project is great as either a shawl or a baby blanket!

"Daylily," designed by author and knitted by Jenni Lesniak

Skill Level: Experienced ◇ ◇ ◇ ◇
Finished Measurements: 56" diameter

MATERIALS

5 balls of Capretta from Knit Picks (80% merino wool, 10% cashmere, 10% nylon; 50 g; 230 yds) in color Hunter (1)
US size 5 (3.75 mm) double-pointed needles, or size needed to obtain gauge
US size 5 (3.75 mm) circular needle, 24" cable, or size needed to obtain gauge
US size 5 (3.75 mm) circular needle, 32" cable or longer, or size needed to obtain gauge
1 stitch marker
Tapestry needle
Flexible blocking wires and/or blocking pins

GAUGE

20 sts and 24 rows = 4" in St st

PATTERN NOTES

Charts A, B, C, D, and E are on page 71. If you prefer to follow written instructions for the charted material, see "Written Instructions for Charts" on page 69.

If using stitch markers to mark each pattern repeat, on some rows the markers will have to be rearranged. For chart A, the markers will move on rows 1, 3, and 5. For chart C, the markers will move on row 9. See page 6 for more information on how to move the markers.

Instructions include "AT THE SAME TIME" directions for moving stitch marker for the start of some rounds. Take care not to miss those!

INSTRUCTIONS

Begin shawl by working set-up rows as follows.

With DPNs and using circular cast on (page 77), CO 9 sts. Join sts and PM to mark start of rnd.

Knit 1 rnd.

Inc rnd: (YO, K1) around. (18 sts)

Knit 2 rnds.

Inc rnd: K1, M1, K10, M1, knit to end of rnd. (20 sts)

Section 1

8 rounds

Inc rnd: (YO, K1) around. (40 sts)

Next rnd: Knit all sts.

Work chart A, while AT THE SAME TIME, on even rnds, remove marker at end of rnd, K1, PM, this marks new start of rnd.

Section 2

16 rounds

Inc rnd: (YO, K1) around. (80 sts)

Next rnd: Knit all sts.

Work chart B.

Section 3

32 rounds

Note: Transfer to 24" circular needle when there are too many stitches on the DPNs.

Inc rnd: (YO, K1) around. (160 sts)

Next rnd: Knit all sts.

Work chart C 3 times, while AT THE SAME TIME, on rnd 8 of chart C, remove marker at end of rnd, K1, PM, this marks new start of rnd.

Section 4

50 rounds

Note: Transfer to 32" or longer circular needle when there are too many stitches on the 24" circular needle.

Inc rnd: (YO, K1) around. (320 sts)

Next rnd: Knit all sts.

Work chart D 4 times.

Section 5

41 rounds

Inc rnd: (YO, K1) around. (640 sts)

Next rnd: Knit all sts.

Work chart E 9 times. Work rnds 1–3 of chart E once more.

> ### Make It Bigger!
>
> With extra yarn, chart E can be repeated to desired length.

FINISHING

BO loosely knitwise as described on page 77. With tapestry needle, weave in ends. Using flexible blocking wires or pins, block to finished measurements.

WRITTEN INSTRUCTIONS FOR CHARTS

If you prefer to follow row-by-row written instructions rather than a chart, use the instructions below.

Chart A

Rnd 1: *K3, YO, K1, YO, K3, sk2p; rep from * around.

Rnds 2 and 4: Knit all sts. At end of rnd, remove marker, K1, PM to mark new start of rnd.

Rnd 3: *K2, YO, K3, YO, K2, sk2p; rep from * around.

Rnd 5: *(K1, YO) twice, sk2p, (YO, K1) twice, sk2p; rep from * around.

Rnd 6: Knit all sts. At end of rnd, remove marker, K1, PM to mark new start of rnd.

Rep rnds 1–6 for patt.

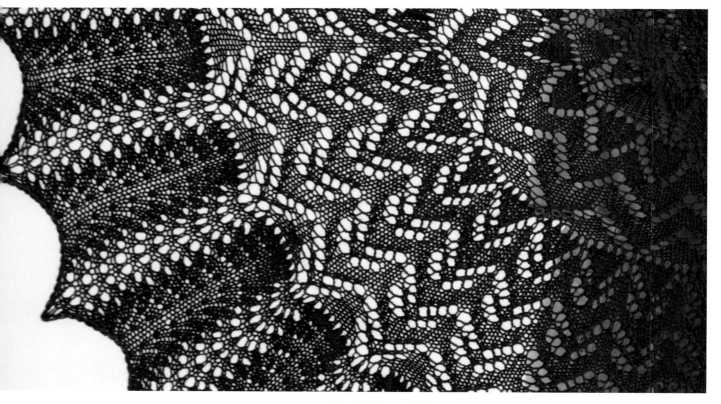

The feather and fan pattern gives the shawl a beautiful pointed edge.

Chart B

Rnd 1: *YO, ssk, K2tog, YO, K1; rep from * around.

Rnd 2 and all even-numbered rnds: Knit all sts.

Rnd 3: *K1, YO, ssk, K3, K2tog, YO, K2; rep from * around.

Rnd 5: *K2, YO, ssk, K1, K2tog, YO, K3; rep from * around.

Rnd 7: *K3, YO, sk2p, YO, K4; rep from * around.

Rnds 9, 11, and 13: *Ssk, K2, YO, K1, YO, K2, K2tog, K1; rep from * around.

Rnd 14: Knit all sts.

Rep rnds 1–14 for patt.

Chart C

Rnd 1: *K4, YO, ssk, K4; rep from * around.

Rnds 2, 4, and 6: Knit all sts.

Rnd 3: *K2, K2tog, YO, K1, YO, ssk, K3; rep from * around.

Rnd 5: *K1, K2tog, YO, K3, YO, ssk, K2; rep from * around.

Rnd 7: *K2tog, YO, K5, YO, ssk, K1; rep from * around.

Rnd 8: Knit all sts. At end of rnd, remove marker, K1, PM to mark new start of rnd.

Rnd 9: *YO, K7, YO, sk2p; rep from * around.

Rnd 10: Knit all sts.

Rep rnds 1–10 for patt.

Chart D

Rnd 1: *YO, ssk, K5, K2tog, YO, K1; rep from * around.

Rnd 2 and all even-numbered rnds: Knit all sts.

Rnd 3: *K1, YO, ssk, K3, K2tog, YO, K2; rep from * around.

Rnd 5: *K2, YO, ssk, K1, K2tog, YO, K3; rep from * around.

Rnd 7: *K1, YO, ssk, YO, sk2p, YO, K2tog, YO, K2; rep from * around.

Rnd 9: *K2, YO, ssk, K1, K2tog, YO, K3; rep from * around.

Rnd 11: *K3, YO, sk2p, YO, K4; rep from * around.

Rnd 12: Knit all sts.

Rep rnds 1–12 for patt.

Chart E

Rnds 1 and 2: Knit all sts.

Rnd 3: *K2tog 3 times, (K1, YO) 6 times, K1, ssk 3 times, K1; rep from * around.

Rnd 4: Knit all sts.

Rep rnds 1–4 for patt.

Daylily Chart A

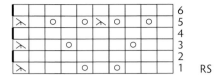

Daylily Chart B

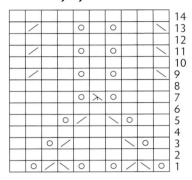

Daylily Chart C

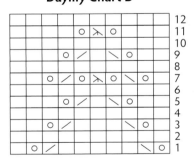

Daylily Chart D

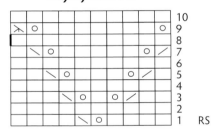

Daylily Chart E

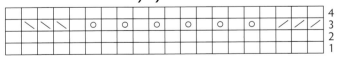

Legend

▢	K on RS, P on WS	◣	Ssk
⊙	YO	◢	K2tog
⋌	Sk2p	▍	Remove marker, K1, PM

SUNBURST

Who doesn't love a multicolored striped shawl? With garter stitch, lace, and stripes, you can't go wrong!

"Sunburst," designed and knitted by author

Skill Level: Experienced ◇ ◇ ◇ ◇
Finished Measurements: 25" x 84"

MATERIALS

Breathless from Shalimar Yarns (75% superwash merino, 15% cashmere, 10% silk; 100 g; 420 yds) **1**

- **A** 1 skein in color Antique
- **B** 1 skein in color Buttermilk
- **C** 1 skein in color Citrine

US size 4 (3.5 mm) circular needle, 32" cable or longer, or size needed to obtain gauge

Tapestry needle

Blocking wires and/or blocking pins

GAUGE

20 sts and 24 rows = 4" in garter st

PATTERN NOTES

The chart is on page 75. If you prefer to follow written instructions for the charted material, see "Written Instructions for Chart" on page 74.

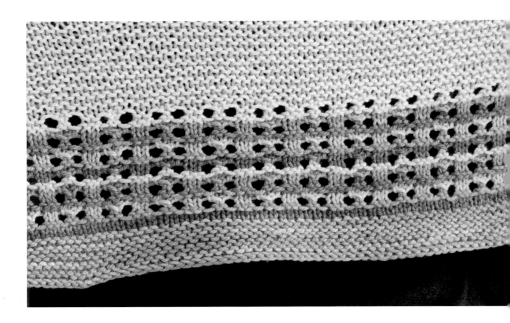

INSTRUCTIONS

Begin shawl by working set-up rows as follows.

With A, CO 5 sts.

Row 1 (WS): (K1, K1f&b) twice, K1. (7 sts)

Row 2 (RS): K2, (YO, K1) 3 times, YO, K2. (11 sts)

Rows 3–5: K2, YO, knit to last 2 sts, YO, K2. (17 sts after row 5)

Garter-Stitch Section A

Cont with A.

Row 1 (RS): K2, YO, K2, M1L, knit to last 4 sts, M1R, K2, YO, K2.

Rows 2–4: K2, YO, knit to last 2 sts, YO, K2.

Work rows 1–4 another 8 times. (107 sts)

Rep row 1 once more. (111 sts)

Next row (WS): K2, YO, knit to last 4 sts, M1R, K2, YO, K2. (114 sts)

Striped Section A

Work chart 5 times total. (264 sts)

Stitch Count	
First rep of chart	144 sts
Second rep of chart	174 sts
Third rep of chart	204 sts
Fourth rep of chart	234 sts
Fifth rep of chart	264 sts

Garter-Stitch Section B

With B only, work as foll:

Row 1 (RS): K2, YO, K2, M1L, knit to last 4 sts, M1R, K2, YO, K2.

Rows 2–4: K2, YO, knit to last 2 sts, YO, K2.

Work rows 1–4 another 5 times. (324 sts)

Striped Section B

Work chart 2 times total.

Stitch Count	
First rep of chart	354 sts
Second rep of chart	384 sts

Garter-Stitch Edge

With C only, work as foll:

Row 1 (RS): K2, YO, K2, M1L, knit to last 4 sts, M1R, K2, YO, K2.

Rows 2–4: K2, YO, knit to last 2 sts, YO, K2.

Work rows 1–4 another 2 times. (414 sts)

Make It Bigger!

If you want the final garter-stitch section to be longer, repeat rows 1–4 as many times as desired.

FINISHING

BO loosely knitwise as described on page 77. With tapestry needle, weave in ends. Using blocking wires or pins, block to finished measurements.

WRITTEN INSTRUCTIONS FOR CHART

If you prefer to follow row-by-row written instructions rather than a chart, use the instructions below.

Row 1 (RS): With B, K2, YO, K2, M1L, K3, *K1, YO, sk2p, YO, K1; rep from * to last 7 sts, K3, M1R, K2, YO, K2.

Row 2 (WS): With B, K2, YO, knit to last 2 sts, YO, K2.

Row 3: With C, K2, YO, knit to last 2 sts, YO, K2.

Row 4: With C, K2, YO, purl to last 2 sts, YO, K2.

Row 5: With A, K2, YO, K2, M1L, K3, *K1, YO, sk2p, YO, K1; rep from * to last 7 sts, K3, M1R, K2, YO, K2.

Row 6: With A, K2, YO, knit to last 2 sts, YO, K2.

Row 7: With B, K2, YO, knit to last 2 sts, YO, K2.

Row 8: With B, K2, YO, purl to last 2 sts, YO, K2.

Row 9: With C, K2, YO, K2, M1L, K3, *K1, YO, sk2p, YO, K1; rep from * to last 7 sts, K3, M1R, K2, YO, K2.

Row 10: With C, K2, YO, knit to last 2 sts, YO, K2.

Row 11: With A, K2, YO, knit to last 2 sts, YO, K2.

Row 12: With A, K2, YO, purl to last 2 sts, YO, K2.

Rep rows 1–12 for patt.

Sunburst Chart

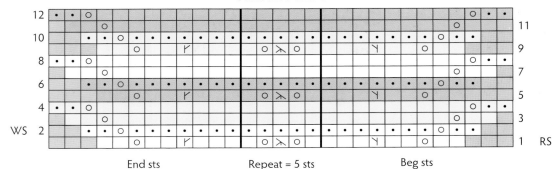

End sts Repeat = 5 sts Beg sts

Legend

☐ K on RS, P on WS with B	▨ K on RS, P on WS with A	☐ K on RS, P on WS with C
⊙ YO with B	⊙ YO with A	⊙ YO with C
Y M1L with B	Y M1L with A	Y M1L with C
⋋ Sk2p with B	⋋ Sk2p with A	⋋ Sk2p with C
Γ M1R with B	Γ M1R with A	Γ M1R with C
• P on RS, K on WS with B	• P on RS, K on WS with A	• P on RS, K on WS with C
▨ No stitch		

Resources

Refer to websites of the following companies to find retail shops that carry yarns featured in this book.

Dragonfly Fibers
www.dragonflyfibers.com
Djinni Sock

Fiesta Yarns
www.fiestayarns.com
Baby Boom

Hazel Knits
www.hazelknits.com
Entice MCN
Divine

Huckleberry Knits
www.etsy.com/shop/huckleberryknits
BFL Sock

Knit Picks
www.knitpicks.com
Capretta

Madelinetosh
www.madelinetosh.com
Tosh Sock

Shalimar Yarns
www.shalimaryarns.com
Breathless

String Theory Hand Dyed Yarn
www.stringtheoryyarn.com
Caper Sock

Three Irish Girls
www.threeirishgirls.com
Adorn Sock

Twisted Fiber Art
www.twistedfiberart.com
Muse

Special Techniques

The following techniques are used throughout the book and will help you successfully knit your shawls.

CAST ONS

For the projects in this book, the following cast ons are used.

Tab Cast On

Several shawls in this book begin with a tab cast on. This cast on is typically written as follows: CO 3 sts, Knit 6 rows.

Rotate work clockwise 90° and pick up three stitches evenly along the edge. *Try to insert the needle into each of the three bumps on the edge of the tab.*

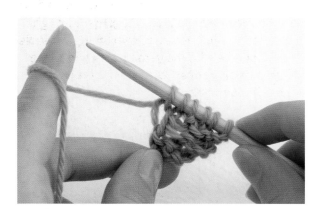

Rotate work clockwise 90° and pick up three stitches evenly from the cast-on edge (9 stitches total). Turn your work and continue with row 1 of the pattern.

Knitted Cast On

Use this cast on to add extra stitches to a shawl, typically when working a border. Start with a slipknot on the left-hand needle. Insert the right-hand needle into the slipknot as if to knit, yarn over, and pull a loop through. Transfer the new stitch from the right-hand needle to the left-hand needle.

Knit into the last stitch on the left-hand needle and transfer the new stitch back to the left-hand needle until you have the correct number of stitches.

Circular Cast On

This cast on is perfect for circular shawls that are worked from the center outward. Once pulled tight, this cast on closes the hole at the center of the shawl. Start by crossing the yarn over itself to make a loose knot. The tail will be on the right side and the working yarn on the left side.

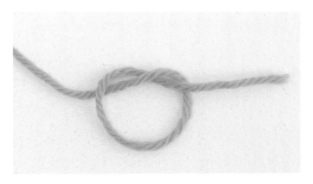

With the working yarn in your left hand, use the right-hand needle to go into the knot, yarn over, and pull a loop through.

Yarn over above the hole to make your next stitch.

Repeat the last two steps, working into the knot and above the knot until you have the desired number of stitches.

Once you start your shawl and work a few rounds, tug on the tail to pull the hole closed. I made a video demonstrating the circular cast on. To view it, visit my website at JenLucasDesigns.com or ShopMartingale.com/HowtoKnit.

BIND OFFS

The goal is to have a stretchy bind off so that when you block your shawl, you can pull and form the edge any way you like. The following knitwise and purlwise bind offs work great.

If you tend to bind off tightly, try using a needle one or two sizes larger. You will be glad you did—you'll be able to pull out the edge of the shawl, creating beautiful points that accent the lace.

Knitwise Bind Off

When binding off on the right side of the work or following garter stitch, use the knitwise bind off. To work, knit the first two stitches together through the back loop. *Slip the stitch from the right needle to the left needle with the yarn in back and K2tog through the back loops; repeat from * until all stitches are bound off.

Purlwise Bind Off

When binding off on the wrong side of the work, use the purlwise bind off: *P2tog, slip stitch from the right needle to the left needle with the yarn in front; repeat from * until all stitches have been bound off, ending with P2tog.

BLOCKING

Soak the shawl in warm water, adding a wool wash if you like. After soaking 15 to 20 minutes, remove and ring it out with a towel. Use either blocking wires or pins to block it to the specified size. For a triangular shawl, I like to run a wire along the top edge, and then carefully stretch it out and pin the wires in place on a blocking board to dry. (If you don't have a blocking board, pin the stretched-out lace to a carpeted floor.) For the side edges, run a wire through the points you want to pull out, and then carefully stretch out the lace and pin the wires in place. For nontriangular shawls, either use a variety of wires at different angles or pin each point individually.

Knitting Abbreviations

( ) Work instructions within parentheses as many times as directed.

* Repeat instructions following the single asterisk as directed.

beg begin(ning)

BO bind off

A color A

B color B

C color C

cm centimeter(s)

cn cable needle(s)

CO cast on

cont continue(ing)(s)

dec(s) decrease(ing)(s)

DPN(s) double-pointed needle(s)

foll follows

g gram(s)

inc(s) increase(ing)(s)

K knit

K1f&b knit in front and back of same stitch—1 stitch increased

K2tog knit 2 stitches together—1 stitch decreased

K3tog knit 3 stitches together—2 stitches decreased

LH left hand

m meter(s)

M1 make 1 stitch—1 stitch increased

M1R with left-hand needle, pick up bar between needles, bringing needle from back to front, and knit into front of stitch—1 stitch increased

M1L with left-hand needle, pick up bar between needles, bringing needle from front to back, and knit into back of stitch—1 stitch increased

mm millimeter(s)

oz ounce(s)

P purl

P2tog purl 2 stitches together—1 stitch decreased

PM place marker

rem remain(ing)

rep(s) repeat(s)

RH right hand

rnd(s) round(s)

RS right side(s)

sk skip

sk2p slip 1 stitch, knit 2 stitches together, pass slipped stitch over the knit 2 together—2 stitches decreased

sl slip

SM slip marker

ssk slip 2 stitches knitwise, 1 at a time, to right needle, then insert left needle from left to right into front loops and knit 2 stitches together—1 stitch decreased

sssk slip 3 stitches knitwise, 1 at a time, to right needle, then insert left needle from left to right into front loops and knit 3 stitches together—2 stitches decreased

st(s) stitch(es)

St st(s) stockinette stitch(es)

tbl through back loop(s)

tog together

WS wrong side(s)

wyib with yarn in back

yd(s) yard(s)

YO(s) yarn over(s)

Useful Information

Yarn-Weight Symbol and Category Name	**1** Super Fine	**2** Fine	**3** Light	**4** Medium	**5** Bulky	**6** Super Bulky
Types of Yarn in Category	Sock, Fingering, Baby	Sport, Baby	DK, Light Worsted	Worsted, Afghan, Aran	Chunky, Craft, Rug	Bulky, Roving
Knit Gauge Range* in Stockinette Stitch to 4"	27 to 32 sts	23 to 26 sts	21 to 24 sts	16 to 20 sts	12 to 15 sts	6 to 11 sts
Recommended Needle in US Size Range	1 to 3	3 to 5	5 to 7	7 to 9	9 to 11	11 and larger
Recommended Needle in Metric Size Range	2.25 to 3.25 mm	3.25 to 3.75 mm	3.75 to 4.5 mm	4.5 to 5.5 mm	5.5 to 8 mm	8 mm and larger

SKILL LEVELS

◇ ◇ ◇ ◇ **Beginner:** Projects for first-time knitters using basic knit and purl stitches; minimal shaping.

◇ ◇ ◇ ◇ **Easy:** Projects using basic stitches, repetitive stitch patterns, and simple color changes; simple shaping and finishing.

◇ ◇ ◇ ◇ **Intermediate:** Projects using a variety of stitches, such as basic cables and lace, simple intarsia, and techniques for double-pointed needles and knitting in the round; mid-level shaping and finishing.

◇ ◇ ◇ ◇ **Experienced:** Projects using advanced techniques and stitches, such as short rows, Fair Isle, more intricate intarsia, cables, lace patterns, and numerous color changes.

METRIC CONVERSIONS

Yards	=	meters	x	1.09
Meters	=	yards	x	0.91
Ounces	=	grams	x	0.035
Grams	=	ounces	x	28.35

KNITTING NEEDLE SIZES

US Size	Size in Millimeters
1	2.25 mm
2	2.75 mm
3	3.25 mm
4	3.5 mm
5	3.75 mm
6	4 mm
7	4.5 mm
8	5 mm
9	5.5 mm
10	6 mm
10½	6.5 mm
11	8 mm
13	9 mm
15	10 mm
17	12.75 mm
19	15 mm
35	19 mm
50	25 mm

About the Author

Acknowledgments

The saying "Team Effort" is definitely true when it comes to this book. I am so lucky to be surrounded by positive, encouraging people who helped me immensely along the way.

My deepest thanks to my sample knitters: Jenni Lesniak, Beth Klein, Gail Nebl, Cathy Rusk, Melissa Rusk, Jennifer Sinnott, and Vickie Zinnel. There would be no shawls in the book without you! I also want to thank Laura Krzak. You may not have done any sample knitting (because you are a crocheter), but your suggestions and encouragement were invaluable to this project.

Thank you to Martingale. You are some of the most kind, supportive people I have met in the industry, and I look forward to continuing to work with you.

Most importantly, I would like to thank my husband, Alex. Your support as I take the plunge into this new career is the best gift you ever gave me.

Thank you all so much. I could not have done this without you.

JEN LUCAS has been knitting since 2004 and designing since 2008. She has had patterns published with Kolláge Yarns as well as Knit Simple and Classic Elite Yarns. Jen also has a growing number of self-published patterns available on Ravelry. Her designs include socks, shawls, and a variety of accessories.

When not knitting, Jen can be found at her spinning wheel, cooking, or pinning Crock-Pot recipes on Pinterest. She lives in Fox River Grove, Illinois, with her husband, Alex.

FIND JEN ONLINE!

See Jen's designs at: www.ravelry.com/designers/jen-lucas

Check out Jen's website at: www.jenlucasdesigns.com

Follow Jen on Twitter: @knitlikecrazy